The Making of a Jamaican Don

Spanner's Views on Dons, Corrupt
Politicians, and Public Officials

Clifton Cameron

iUniverse, Inc.
New York   Bloomington

The Making of a Jamaican Don

iUniverse books may be ordered through booksellers or by contacting:

iUniverse
1663 Liberty Drive
Bloomington, IN 47403
www.iuniverse.com
1-800-Authors (1-800-288-4677)

Because of the dynamic nature of the Internet, any Web addresses or
links contained in this book may have changed since publication and
may no longer be valid. The views expressed in this work are solely those
of the author and do not necessarily reflect the views of the publisher,
and the publisher hereby disclaims any responsibility for them.

ISBN: 978-1-4502-7046-5 (sc)
ISBN: 978-1-4502-7047-2 (dj)
ISBN: 978-1-4502-7048-9 (ebook)

Library of Congress Control Number: 2010916499

Printed in the United States of America

iUniverse rev. date: 11/11/2010

Preface

Most of the names of the characters in this book are entirely fictional as are some of the events described. However, most aspects within the book are taken from personal experiences in Jamaica. Spanner tells his story from personal experience he had on the street of Kingston and during his time campaigning with various political candidates on both side of the political fences. Lots of feathers will be ruffled but it's time the truth be told, no matter what it cost, Jamaica deserve better. It's time to say no to don culture and corrupt public officials.

My name is Clifton Cameron, a Jamaican but now residing in the United Kingdom. I was born and grew up in Saint Catherine, in a little district called Old Road near Kitson Town. As a child I attended the Guanaboa Vale All Age School. During my school days I was a good child who always attended school, and I was good at athletics and my schoolwork. My interest in writing started while attending school in Guanaboa Vale and learning about Shakespearian poetry. That's where I got my vibes from to write my first book of inspirational poetry called (**Voice from the Wilderness**). The Making of a Jamaican Don' is my second book and it's a true story about two young men, Spanner and Trinity from rural Jamaica, who went to Kingston to make a better life for themselves and ended up in the criminal underworld. Sylvan is Spanner and Errol is Trinity two of the characters that played out in this book.

I too was raised by my grandmother from the age of five months after I was given to her by my mother. My granny was the most loving old lady and everyone loved her. During my years living with my granny, I grew up in a big extended family with uncles, aunties and lots of cousins. I wasn't short of anything while growing up; the property was very fruitful with all type of fruits and there was always food to eat. On my grandmother property she has lots of coffee and I would always help her to pick the fruits ever week for sale to the trucks that come to collect the coffee.

As a boy growing up I always liked storytelling, and while in the UK, I found out that I had a talent, and there, and then I decided to write poetry, short stories and other kind writing. Having a focus in life helps me to challenge my energy into writing. I didn't get the chance to graduate from school, but grew up fast and I learn everything on the street.

The book is base on a true story on real life situation with Trinity

1

and Spanner who went off to Kingston searching for a better life. They both have different goals but ended up in a life of crime. They both went to prison in Jamaica, America and the United Kingdom. After leaving prison they both embarked on fulfilling their dreams of becoming rich.

Just to inform everyone who might be wondering who Spanner was: Spanner is Sylvan the little boy with the dog and the bottle torch, the same little boy who follows his grandmother with her load to meet the bus. Spanner was the same little boy who helps his grandmother picked the fruits and he was also in the bus the morning while the bus was being loaded.

Errol is Trinity, one of the nine guys on the bus who went to Kingston to look for work. (Bunty Killer is a famous Jamaican reggae DJ, also known on the dancehall scene as the war Lord.) When you read about bird, it's what people called a prison sentence. Example: Zekes is now serving a long sentence in prison.

Spanner involvement in IT

It was by chance Spanner was sent to an IT company one day as a hit man to collect JA$500,000 that was owed to his friend. On entering the office and seeing the type of work that was going on in the building, Spanner got interested. He asked to see the boss and was taken to an office where the boss was sitting around his desk. The clerk returned to her desk and closes the door behind her. Spanner told the boss what he was there for and the boss told him that he didn't had any money but he would make sure the money was ready by Friday. Spanner lifts up his shirt and showed the boss the handle of his pistol and told him that he was told to kill him if he didn't get the money.

The boss pleads for his life and offer Spanner the fifty US dollar he had in his wallet. He told Spanner to take the money as a gift, and that the coming Friday he would get the money. The two men chatted for a while about computers and the boss offer to give Spanner a tour of the building to the many different departments. Spanner didn't like the programming section where they build website and write programs, but when the boss took him to the Hardware department where they build, repair, and upgraded computers and cabling, he was delighted. He fell in love with the computers, so he asked if one day he could return to learn the trade and to his surprise he was offered the opportunity. Spanner was a very considerate person and he like the boss after getting to know him so there was no way he was going to hurt a person who genuinely wants to help him.

Spanner was an enforcer and an illegal debt collector but after meeting the owner of the IT Company, his priority changed. He was no more interested in that kind of work so he didn't go back to the office as a debt collector but as a trainee PC technician. Soon Spanner would be traveling with the other workers all over Jamaica working in Banks, Schools, Government Ministries and other businesses, building computer laboratory and fixing computers. Spanner was by now enjoying building PCs, laying cables and doing up computer lab. It wasn't long before he would be hooked on the internet. He loved the internet so much, that the boss called him 'browser'. By now Spanner was very close to the boss and he would go to the office every morning at 7.am and he would browse the internet until 8.30am when it was time to do the boss work.

Spanner reflecting on his earlier days in crime

Spanner should and could have represented Jamaica in athletics but somewhere along the way he got side tracked and started to get into trouble after his loving grandfather died. Fighting was a regular thing after the death of his grand dad and it would get him into trouble with the police. His grandmother was left alone to take care of him. Maybe he was missing his grandfather and that was what caused Spanner to get off the rail. The Guanaboa Vale police station was a few metres from his school and every time the cops came to the school to arrest Spanner, he would get away. He always had friends looking out for him and they would inform him when the cops were coming to catch him. The police at Guanaboa Vale are like shepherd who take cares of the cows on Adrian property.

While growing up Spanner had lots of laying fowls that were given to him by his godmother's friend (Miss B, who lives at Pedro District) as a birthday present, he was good with animals. He started with one chicken and it quickly provided him with dozens of chickens. He also had a goat by the name of Betty that was given to him by his grandfather, the goat always produced three kids from every pregnancy, until one day it strayed onto a wicked man's land and she was poisoned. Spanner cried for weeks, and vowed that when he became a man he would seek revenge for the death of his goat. He was only seven years old at the time and from there on he started to get into trouble.

Spanner eventually got his revenge on the man by taking his new Honda motor cycle and running away to Kingston with it where he stayed with some people he had made friends with for little over a year. Those people that Spanner stopped with were hardened criminals; they scrapped the bike and sold the parts. Spanner was only given a pair of pants and a few dollars out of the money that they received from the bike parts that were sold. One of the guys who robbed Spanner was called 'Duppy' he was an ugly man, with a huge head and scars all over his face. He looked like someone who had fought many battles on the streets of Kingston. Spanner wasn't going to tolerate his bike being taken away from him without doing something about it. Spanner was fourteen years at the time that incident happened in 1977.

One night while the main culprit who took his bike was asleep, he was shot in his heart with a nail gun and his house burned down with his body still in it. Spanner returned to Kitson Town to live, where he resided until 1980. It was in 1981 Spanner returned to Kingston to live in Water House with his brother. During that time, Spanner made a name for himself and moved up in the criminal underworld. He was feared in Marvaley, Drewsland, Samakan, Buckers, Binns Road, Cuba, Wailers, Sea View Garden, Olympic Garden and Riverton City. All those area are located in Kingston 11, excluding Marvaley, Drewsland and Samakan. It was while living in Water House aka Fire House that Spanner was charged for murder and was sent to GP. In 1990, he was released on parole and the rest was history.

Historical facts on Jamaican Dons and Wanted men

Tree Fingered Jack

In the 18th century, there was a rebellious slave named Jack Mansong; his friends called him 'Three Fingered Jack' and he was a real warrior. He fled the plantation -where he had been forced to live-for the mountains, where he became a menace to the white slave masters. Of course, we all know that the slave masters were British and Scottish and that's how the majority of Jamaicans got their names from. Three, Fingered Jack was so skilful at evading capture that the British slave masters branded him an outcast and a bandit, and they placed a £300 bounty on his head. Mansong made one unsuccessful attempt at killing one of the slave traders which caused an island wide manhunt for him. After many months of evading the manhunt, he was captured, jailed and sentenced to death.

Three, Fingered Jack was full of surprises; so on the night before his execution he escaped. That wasn't enough though, so he kidnapped one of the slave masters's and held him captive in the Saint Thomas hills in one of his many hide out where there were many caves. The slave traders were fuming and questioning how could that happened especially when they were all armed with guns. Despite being organised, they couldn't capture Jack, so they sought the help of another slave to capture and kill him. This slave, who got the contract to kill his fellow slave, was a Maroon. It's a well known fact that the Jamaican maroons were informers because they worked with the white slave masters against their own fellow slaves.

Quashie was the name of the traitor slave who tracked down Mansong and shot him dead. Perhaps he got his £300 just like Judas got his thirty pieces of silver for selling out Christ (I wonder if he hung himself like Judas did?). It was over 200 years ago since 'Three Fingered Jack's' death, he was the first wanted man in Jamaica since records began. Since his death, over two centuries ago, hundreds if not thousands of criminals have been on Jamaica's most wanted lists. Jack was the victim of the cruel system of slavery, but modern Jamaican dons and wanted men are the product of corrupt politicians and the injustices of Jamaica justice system. The Jamaican police are judges, jury and executioners, this breeds contempt and resentment, and hence the revenge culture continues in a destructive path.

Claudie Massop and Bucky Marshal

As the political tribalism grew, so did the role of the area leader. Claudius 'Claudie' Massop was a (JLP) don and Aston 'Bucky' Marshall was a (PNP) don who all came to national prominence in the 1970s. They played a major role in peace initiatives such as the One Love Peace

Concert in April 1978. It was during that period of national unrest, the modern day don really started taking shape.

"These dons were under the patronage of the politicians, and they began to travel to the United States where they started to made their own contacts," "The drug trade wasn't that hard to get into so it open up their eyes to the world and they started getting independent of their parties while getting rich in their drugs activities."

By the 1980s and 1990s, the don's transcended into drugs running and smuggling of guns. Many got involved in the entertainment business as producers or show promoters; others got security and construction contracts from politicians and building contractors, allegedly through their ties with Government. Dons benefit from the extortion racket, raking in millions of dollars from the 'protection' of businessmen in some of Jamaica's thriving commercial districts.

Don ship no longer existed only in urban areas; it's now in St. James, Spanish Town, Clarendon and Westmoreland and in all other parishes in a lesser extent. All dons operate off the same ethos that is used in Kingston and it's usually linked to the drugs trade and corrupt politicians. Over the years, many dons including Massop, Marshall, Starkey, Feathermop, died violently.

Dennis Barth aka Copper

Of all the modern day wanted men, Copper was the most dangerous. 'Dennis Copper Barth' was a legend who was the leader of the East Kingston based 'Hot Stepper' gang. He and his group of outlaws were experts at robbing banks and he was a cold-blooded killer who was a master at his game. Police used to shiver and wet their pants when they heard Coppers name mentioned in any robbery. The police can testify to that, because he really put them in their place, ironically most bad men today are trying to walk in Coppers footsteps. They saw Copper as a don who wasn't afraid of anyone and didn't play with the police. In the 1970s, Trinity and Spanner regarded Copper and the rest of his 'bad boys' with him as role model. They used to watch the news and pray that Copper didn't get caught or killed by the police.

When Copper died in that shoot out over by Caymanas Park Race Track, all dons and admirers were sad. The police on their own couldn't capture Copper, so they got an informer to grass on him so that they could murder him. Why didn't they take him in alive? Maybe the informer was a maroon too? Copper was killed in 1978 and it was no surprise on who collected that JA $5,000 bounty on his head. (Some of Jamaica's most senior cops would admitted that Copper wasn't afraid to take on the police at anytime with impunity). He was captured in Tivoli Gardens by a police patrol, which was led by a famous cop, and was able to escape custody two times. Mr Hewitt and Adams can testify to that.

Derrick Adair aka Shabba

The most dangerous don or vile criminal and political enforcer to have ever come out of Jamaica and the politically turbulent decade of the 1970s was Derrick Adair, aka known in the criminal underworld as 'Shabba'.

Shabba was a Jamaica Labour Party (JLP) enforcer and don who were born in the community of Fletcher's Land in downtown Kingston. Although there was no official tally, criminal operatives of that era blamed Shabba for the murders of at least 20 police officers and soldiers. He was a don with a vengeance. Because of his skills as a robber it earned him the respect of former most wanted fugitive Dennis 'Copper' Barth and the two soon became partners in crime.

Sandokan and his revenge on the police

Next on the most wanted list and public enemy number one was Wayne 'Sandokan' Smith from Water House, where Spanner grew up, and knew him. He wasn't as bad as Trinity or Spanner, but after Spanner went to prison and Trinity went to America, Sandokan broke out in the badness world and the rest was history. Sandokan was involved in the planning and execution of a famous attack on the Olympic Garden police station. Spanner was at the General Penitentiary at the time when the attack took place. Rumours had it that the cops disrespected Sandokan's girlfriend by beating her until she saw her period. No man would tolerate a thing like that, even if the person who did it was the Prime Minister of Jamaica or the President of America! He would have to get fixed up, and that was exactly what Sandokan did. Someone had to die for the disrespect and pain the cops caused him and his girl, so Sandokan and his gang paid the police a visit one night.

In 1982, Spanner was taken to Olympic Garden police station and was beaten on his foot bottom, by five criminal police men, until they were swollen and he couldn't walk. Those were some of the things that the Jamaican police did to innocent people and got away with it. This kind of behaviour caused grievance and people carried revenge in their hearts for the police. Spanner was taken to the Hunts Bay police station where he was jailed without charge for two weeks. Beating someone on their feet was the norm at Olympic Garden and Hunts Bay police station during the 1980s, and the reason for that was to hide the evidence in case someone died from their injuries during regular beatings.

Beating someone under their feet, supposedly, hide the cause of death. Hunts Bay and Olympic Garden police were the main culprits in abusing detainee's human rights. It was no wonder some of the police stations got shot up and some of the criminal cops got killed. It was hard to show sympathy for those cops because ironically, they were often the ones who sold the criminals the very same guns and ammunitions that sometimes killed them! Many dons, wanted men, and others who were in GP prison at the same time as Spanner, celebrated over the attack on Olympic Garden police station.

Too many wrongs and injustices was going on, people couldn't get any justice, so someone had to avenge the cops for all the cruelties they perpetrated on hundreds of innocent people all over Jamaica, especially Kingston 11. Sandokan raided the police station with his band of 'merry men'; they killed three policemen and stole guns and ammunition. The whole country was scared, so the government sent out the police and army to capture him. The government never did that though about injustice, when the cops killed innocent citizens! What the Jamaican people didn't know was that the police were the culprits who turned Sandokan into a monster and public enemy number one.

Sandokan was from Water House aka Fire House, a name given to the community because of its bad reputation, he and his gang were in hiding there. He was a gangster and he was frequently in the Riverton area where 'Bounty Killer' originated from. There were many curfews and raids to capture Sandokan but they always failed to catch him. However, he was eventually gunned down in Water House in a place called 'Cuba' in 1989 by P-man, a friend of Spanner. Not long after Sandokan was killed Natty Morgan came on the scene.

Natty Morgan

Natty Morgan was a time bomb waiting to explode and when his time for fame came he took it with both hands. Nathaniel 'Natty' Morgan was the leader of a gang in Kingston 11 where many wanted individuals and dons came from. Natty was ruthless, and was wanted for many murders. He was best remembered for the seven people he executed in Sea View Garden while they were attending the wake of another of his victims. He was captured and sent to the General Penitentiary prison where he was remanded until he attended the notorious Gun Court on South Camp Road. Natty escaped from the gun court prison in 1990 while attending court there. He was placed in a cell during a lunch break but he walked out through the security gate to his freedom. He evaded the law for eight months before he was finally killed.

Before he was killed, he drove fear in the police and the country. He was the type of guy who didn't care or have any fear of the police, bad men or dons. Natty's favorite place was down by Riverton City dump where he was 'king of the castle'. He was a don, and he extorted money from all the big businesses on Spanish Town Road. Natty was one of the most famous fugitives to ever grace Jamaica because of the severity of his crimes. While hiding away in Lakes Pen in Saint Catherine, he was cornered and killed- execution style- by the police. He too was given away by an informer.

There were many more bad men who got executed by the police and their peers. Spanner once commented that he knew all the gunmen who were linked with most MPs, from Prime Ministers down to councilors on both sides of the political fences. While in GP Prison Spanner got to meet and know most of Jamaica dangerous criminals. Spanner and Trinity were members of the Jamaica Labour Party, even though at one stage Spanner switched sides to the People National Party for a short period.

Spanner often declared how much he loved his country and that he wanted to see politicians properly do their work in the communities that they were elected to represent. If they didn't and he could not get the politicians to do what was right, he maintained that he had no other choice other than to switch to a party that was for the good of the people. He felt politicians were the cause of the crime situation in Jamaica and that all so-called gunmen were members of the two major political parties. Politicians helped to create division in communities, which in turn created dons and no go areas; dons had friends in very high places.

In Jamaica, many so-called dons rarely lived until they became old. Then there are the fugitives, whose life span rarely past three years after they became one of Jamaica's most wanted. The first modern day official record of 'don-man-ship' in Jamaica dates to sometime in September 1948, when the famous Ivanhoe Martin alias 'Rhyging' was killed in Lime Cay by the police in a raging gun battle. This don was so famous that his character was played in the Jimmy Cliff movie, The Harder They Come.

Cedrick Murray, the leader of the 'Stone Crusher' gang, who had been on a list of Jamaica's 10 most wanted men for more than seven years, was one of the longest don on the run in Jamaica.

Politicians and their dons

Edward Seaga was brave enough to drink beer in the glare of television lights with known criminals and enforcers in his constituency, and Michael Manley would feel no compunction in leading a delegation of PNP stalwarts to the funeral of Winston 'Burrey Boy' Blake, head of the PNP-affiliated Garrison Gang.

West Kingston and Central Kingston, was controlled by two former Prime Ministers, who had some of the most ruthless and nefarious political gunmen and terrorists this country has ever seen. But it did not cost Seaga and Manley their seats.

The links between Jamaican politics and criminality are well established and the transaction costs of these links are incalculable. But we must not lose heart. There are still criminals associated with the political parties and criminal gangs still exploiting their party political connections to carry out their illegal activities, like drug-running, but they operate in a social and political environment which has changed significantly and more sophisticated.

Roy Fowl

British Link-up Crew, Owen 'Father Fowl' Clarke is another don who done 13 years in prison in England. As a jerk chicken vendor while living in Kingston, The British authorities said Fowl ran a cocaine empire that raked in millions of British pounds which enabled him to live a life of luxury in the UK and Jamaica.

Father Fowl' ran the British Crew just as Vivian Blake ran the Shower Posse in the United States during the 1980s and 1990s. They represent the new breed of Jamaican dons who have a major influence on this Jamaica's popular culture said most media commentators.

How Don-ship works

Dons are questionable characters who are involved in criminal activities and associated with politicians, business people and even the police. Dons are sometimes classed as area leaders or someone who spoke on behalf of a community even though in most cases they weren't elected by the majority of the people. Dons can be so-called community leaders. A don is like a dictator who rules his community with an iron fist. Dons are people who decides the faith of persons who to get killed, which women to get rape, give out order to kill police and are also the contact person who the politicians seek out for their help in bullying the people into voting for them. Dons are self proclaim individuals who politicians gave contracts as a reward for their loyalty and support for them.

Don's in Jamaica see themselves as leaders, protectors, and most of all 'god'- like figures. They even see themselves bigger than the Prime Minister and with the resources they have today, they are not afraid of anyone. Their reason for thinking like that is because they can get anyone killed if they wanted to. A don is someone who controls vast areas of cities, ghettos and rural areas. They are the ones who give out orders on how their area should be run, and command respect from the people they control through their hench men.

Politicians have to show respect to the dons, and if they don't they may not be able to come in the area or get any votes so the politicians have to pay up or shut up. It must be noted that a don can get any girl living in his area, whether by free will or through force. If the don sees a woman he wants and he can't get her he will send some of his goons to get her and then he would rape her with a gun to her head. After she was rape she would be warned not to go to the police or tell anyone, and if she did, he would kill her or her family if she was caught.

If the woman or girl leaves the area without giving the don the chance to rape her, he would see that as a form of disrespect to him and he could easily get her family killed and then burn down their house. The don of any area in Jamaica is liked god to the people and see himself as untouchable because he can act like the PM (not legally) judge, jury, executioner, godfather and just about anyone he want to be. He can wield his power while ruling his community with an iron fist. The code is that all informers, (grass) should be killed. The community is shut off from the police and people often get killed for talking to the cops. It won't be long before don's start to sanction the killing of politicians.

In those areas the police can't go in unless they have protection from the army. When it comes to calling the police at night many people don't even bother. In some areas the police can't go in them at night because they are so dangerous, so police will tell the caller that they can't help, what a way to serve and protect the public! Not all dons are bad; Spanner was a good don who looked after his community in Kitson Town by helping the people instead of oppressing them. When he was freed from GP, he went through the community and gave out his warnings that there should be no more rape, robbery, shooting or crime in the area. He was an enforcer, and the crime stopped.

The police even thanked Spanner and told him that since he returned there was no more crime and that he had done their work for them. Spanner did not extort money from the businesses in his area, even though most of them offered him cash and food for the security he provided. When Spanner was in prison, there was lots of crime in and around Kitson Town. After Spanner was released and he gave out his warning, crime seemed to stop. There was no raping, murder or stealing going on anymore. Everyone was happy. The police even told Spanner that they knew that he had guns but that was not their problem as long as he didn't let them catch him with any.

Spanner wasn't the kind of guy who liked to take disadvantage of his people, but the other so-called dons were like parasites, they even collected taxes (extortion) from poor people. Maybe that was why they didn't live that long. To be a don you have to be tough or even rough but Spanner was in between.

To Mabrak

This is a tribute to my cousin who was known to everyone across Jamaica and the world as Mabrak or Calabash. He was the best Calabash artist in Jamaica, no one taught him to carve, but he excelled at his craft. Mabrak was Spanners 'teacher' and cousin, and he was the first person to get Spanner involved in politics. He taught Spanner to shoot birds and swim in the river at Guanaboa Vale. Mabrak was a warrior and Spanner always remembered what he had taught him. In 2008 some coward murdered Mabrak, but his memory still lives on. May God bless his soul and may he rest in peace. R.I.P Mabrak.

The Dudus Saga

I remember when Dudus started getting his fame, and one day Spanner and Trinity stopped by number seven Chesnut Lane to pick up a German Luger automatic pistol. Dudus had heard about Trinity's arrival in the area and requested for Trinity to report to him over in Tivoli Garden. Trinity wasn't interested in seeing him because he didn't think he was in his category much more to pay him taxes. Dudus didn't really know who Trinity and Spanner were, but, after making enquires he found out they were friends of his father and they had all spent time in GP. After finding out that Spanner and Trinity had been associates of his dad he didn't bother to make a fuss.

Spanner used to live in West Kingston during the 1970s and knew most of the original bad men who later became dons for Tivoli, Reama and so forth. Dudus was nobody back then, but after the death of his father, brother Jah T and his sister, he rose to fame. This didn't happen overnight, because if the politicians, Councillors and MP for West Kingston weren't in agreement with the governance of Tivoli Garden, Jamaica wouldn't have to witnessed the two invasions that cost over one hundred innocent lives. Not all people who live in Garden are criminal but many are in agreement with the don mentality which sometimes works more effectively than the legal establishment. Just checkout (Passa-Passa) and see how the place is well organised. No crime can commit in Tivoli unless it's sanction by who control the security of the area.

Trinity wasn't someone to play with, and perhaps Dudus had realised this during his enquires. After the gun was handed over they left the area, but on their way toward Kitson Town, Trinity remarks was that if Dudus did ever disrespected him he would have the whole of his family killed. Dudus must have smelled a rat, because he found out that he was dealing with a more powerful man than himself. With the resources Trinity had, he could get anything done by the click of his fingers.

Spanner remarks were "you should have seen Dudus face when the Feds were escorting him to prison in America? He was like a scared little boy witting his pant. Looking at his picture, it was hard to believe that he was the don who ruled Tivoli with an iron fist". He was like a lamb to the slaughter and I felt his pain. You would have to be a real rude boy to understand what I am talking about. Being taking from your country by some punk without firing a shot or killing some agent make the underworld community sick in their stomach.

It was not unusual to get help from gunmen from other areas when protecting ones turf, if you command the respect. As the president of West Kingston, Dudus acted cowardly when he ran away and left his soldiers who were dying defending him. What happened in Garden was cold blooded murder. There was no way he could have so many so-called gunmen defending him as the police and government said, and only one soldier got killed. Spanner questioned: "who are they trying to fool with their lies? They think that poor people are stupid, they can feed the press with their propaganda but Jamaicans are no fools." With so many machine guns, as reported, it would be very difficult for the police and soldiers to get into Tivoli without many of them getting killed?"

Numerous forces inimical to Jamaica were revealed in the Dudus saga, including America and the United Kingdom. Conscious Jamaicans considered the New World Order and its implications toward Jamaica. Perhaps the US destabilisation of Jamaica seemed like child's play to Washington because Jamaicans worship America and now, President Barack Obama! Blessed Jamaica is perennially envied by "brute beast Euro-Americans," which recently got whipped in international sports by Jamaican athletes. Chaos created in Jamaica and other countries by evil globalist's offered distraction from their own problems. There were dangerous insurgencies raging in the US, especially in the Boston Tea Party Movement, with signs of impending civil war.

That was how the British got booted out of America, because they were taking the Americans for fools but now America was leading the way with its bullying tactics. The Dudus saga was to pressure Jamaica into submission by pressuring the puppet PM and his deputy to hand over Dudus. Seemingly, Mr Golding was not for sale, or was he? All Jamaican Prime Ministers are for sale because they always sell out the country. Although Golding leads the same JLP Judases they always sell out the party that betrayed Jamaica to Reagan's US in the 1980s. Seaga was instrumental in killing out the weed that poor people used to send their children to school; many of whom turning out to be lawyers, doctors, and teachers and so on.

Golding, who now angered Euro-America when he effectively told them, by paraphrasing Mister Fabulous the Reggae DJ: "I man nuh play number two." These types of phrases often mean that he is no batty boy or gay. As in the Roman Empire, playing number two is a priority for the globalists. Jamaica is a beautiful country and there is a conspiracy to see it fail. Jamaica could be better off but none of the criminals who rule it want to see poor people elevate themselves. For some 6000 years, white people have been decimating people of colour. Their drug wars, terror wars and killing of Iraqis, Afghans, and practically all predominantly black people on earth are key pieces of their population reduction plan.

Jamaica is a black country that is being used by Britain and the US. Their endgame is in place, whereby, globalists are ready to decimate their own race to get rid of people who do not share their racist, globalist, satanic views. Some people, like Jamaicans, reject this evil globalism because it offends their faith in God, but many branches of Christianity are leaders in this march to the white supremacist one-world government. Jamaicans must use the spirit of discernment to identify those churches that are Satan's servants, especially churches headquartered in Euro-America.

Weed out Corruption from all Quarters in Jamaica

The worst slave masters Jamaicans could ever have are politicians and business leaders, because they are the ones who oppressed the poor, robbed and squandered the country's resources. Spanner said: "I went to many conferences and executive meetings with politicians and I can tell you that, 'those lot' don't care a hoot about black people. The fact that some of their skin are black doesn't change the fact that they are like the foremen on the white plantation in the days of slavery. They would take the whip from the land owners (who happen to be politicians and business leaders) who are also the American, British and Europeans and punish the poor because they want their masters to like them. This kind of thing happened during the British and Scottish rule and it's happening now in Jamaica in the 21st century. Look at the people who are running the two political parties and the heads of major businesses in Jamaica and tell me what do you see? Those people are all from the upper classes and their skin tones are lighter".

Sad but true: Jamaicans are not capable of governing themselves. After almost half a century of so-called independence which seems more like dependence, Jamaica is worse off than when the original slave masters ruled it. We are like crabs, even in foreign countries Jamaicans fight against themselves. Maybe that is where the divide and rule comes in. Spanner believed that if he had the authority, he would wipe out all Jamaican criminal politicians and replace them with decent law abiding citizens who were patriotic and wanted good for their country; none of the politicians could say that they wanted any good for the country, because he knew them all and what they were up to and that's no good.

Should Jamaica get its independence or should it still be ruled by Britain???

Spanner said, "Personally I don't think Jamaica should have got its independence from Britain at the time it did. My reason for saying so is because at the moment Jamaica cannot govern itself. Now would be the right time for Jamaica to be looking to gain its independence, that is, if it was able to show that it really and truly qualifies to rule its people. During the days of the British rule, Jamaica was administered better, looking at the state of the country now? Everywhere that the British still rule is much better developed than Jamaica. The Jamaican politicians were like wasps, they were short sighted, they couldn't wait and learn how to make honey, instead they can only make the honey comb without any wax or honey, and it run before it could walk. If the pioneers who fought for Jamaica independence had waited a bit longer, then we would have had a well developed country to take over from the British".

"All the social ills we have today would be less, there is no social housing for the people who need it, the national health service is crying out for help, what's the use of free health care when people have to get up out of their sickbeds to queue in line from 3.am in the morning just to get some medicine? The worst thing is that when some of them reach the counter (hours later) only to be told that the medicine has run out. That's not proper governance! There are so many things in Jamaica that need to be fixed, just because our so-called leaders haven't done their homework. If I was fighting for independence, I would see to it that everything was in place, developmental wise before I take over the running of the country. Those earlier leaders made a big error of judgement when they took control of Jamaica's affairs by not seeing what was going to happen in the years to come".

He continued: "Looking at Northern Ireland, once ruled by the British; they fought the British for a long time and in the end they will get their self rule and it is now a well developed country and was promised a £56, 000.000. 000, budget by White Hall. They have over half of million new homes that can be occupied but no one to go into them, in other words the Irish are better off to take control of their country and govern it, and they have all the resources in place, not so in Jamaica. Jamaica wouldn't be in the mess it's in today if the leaders had just waited a few more decades. Ok, so Jamaica got its independence, what happened to all the money that the country got for development over the years? Where did it go? Jamaica has some of the worst roads, which stifle the country's agricultural sector and the politicians do nothing about it. Why not bring in a project where poor people in the country could plant crop and then sell it to the farmer's market that runs by the government? Then the big hotels could come in and buy the local produce and it would be a win, win situation for everyone.

This could help to cushion the joblessness in the rural parts of the country and form a livelihood for the poor people".

Politics in Jamaica is like a club, and the only way an outsider could get in was by licking party official's ass. Some females got in because they had affairs with officials, while the men had to be friends of high ranking officials to get into the club. Some men even have sexual affairs with male party officials to get a seat on the political boat. Spanner hoped that one day the boat would sink with all the parasites and no good politicians who don't mean Jamaica and the poor people any good.

Trinity used the example of three former security ministers from both political parties who gave guns to their constituents to fight politics. Some even ran garrison constituencies. Trinity didn't want to go back to the 1980s, where some of the politicians were themselves shooting at each other's. A politician from Brown's Hall was a victim of a shooting and someone got murdered in the process in Old Harbour. Spanner was a part of the JLP group and was only 17 years old, when that happened and he couldn't vote legally. Spanner had seen so many wrongs but what could he do? The things that hurt him most of all was the way politicians conducted their business. During an election campaign, party supporters had absolute power to do whatever they wanted to whomever they wanted to.

No grants for Jamaica unless Politicians clean up their act, and get rid of corruption.

Spanner said "as a Jamaican, I love my country and its people. I would encourage the donor countries to stop giving Jamaica grants or developmental aid until the corrupt politicians and government clean themselves up and get their act together. No agencies or organisations should give aid to Jamaica unless they have people in the country that can run the projects themselves. That way the aid would reach the people who need it most. No one would get the chance to sell or steal money to enrich themselves. The foreign governments and donor agencies are the ones who are helping the country so it shouldn't be a problem if the donors stipulate that for the funding to go ahead, they should be given control of finances and materials and they should also be responsible for funding, the country should then be given responsibility for finding two thirds of the labour." Spanner continued: "I am so ashamed to see my country, Jamaica, being run by a bunch of criminals."

Spanner once said: "as a former bad boy in Jamaica, I am asking the Commissioner of Police to answer to the people's cry, for an investigation with a view of prosecution to be brought against some public officials, which includes politicians, police, lawyers and some opulent members of the private sector who have links with perpetrators of crimes in connection with guns, corruption, drugs trafficking and extortion." The authorities should be directing it resources In clamping down on corruption and by doing so, hit the so-called big people first and stop pressuring the poor in the ghetto.

The government should be directing scarce resources to the thousands of children and poor people residing below halfway Tree and other areas of that kind throughout Jamaica, why don't they help to develop the ghetto youths by providing them with skills or jobs so that they can earn a decent living by working for their honest bread? To the so-called bakras (and their children), some of whom behave like plantation masters disrespecting the lower classes, as if the ancestors of those innocent children have not suffered enough as victims of the worst form of slavery. It is because of the oppression from those bakras masters why most ghetto youths have to resort to being a don. The people who owned big businesses didn't want to employ so-called 'ghetto people' to work for them, no wonder the ghetto youths had to rob the society people in the hills. Not that Spanner was saying it was right to take what was not yours; he was just making a point.

Cuba, China and Venezuela's Mr Chavez loved Jamaica and given more help than what the US and UK gives together. The UK and USA were only interested in their so-called 'fight against drugs' while not helping Jamaica to build schools and hospitals. In the 1970s, the Cuban gave Jamaica three schools Venezuela gave us the San Jose accord which gave Jamaica oil at small interest rate for many years so that the profit was used by government to develop Portmore community. There was nothing Jamaica could show that the UK and US gave the country to help its people? Maybe guns and speed boats? The European Union did a better job to Jamaica and they weren't the one who slave Jamaican. The Chinese are a people who show their love and commitment to the people of Jamaica. You can see the development that's done by them. Show me what the British and American done?

When the international community gave money to Jamaica, most of it was stolen and not many people benefitted. The Netherlands is another country that did much good for Jamaica. The British government is wicked because after the slave's rebellion against their inhumane rules and treatment, they responded by hanging our fore fathers and branded Jamaicans violent. They hang Paul Bogle, George

William Gordon, Sam Sharp, Taki, Cojoe and many more brave leaders of the Jamaican people. Jamaica is still being badly treated by foreign government who continue to say that Jamaica's people are too violent. Paul Bogle, George William Gordon and Sam Sharpe are now national heroes because of the fight they put up to end slavery. They fought against injustice and the British responded by hanging them.

Don's who disgraced Jamaica and paid the price

Spanner witnessed whilst in GP, Jim Brown being freed of a murder charge at the Circuit (Crown) Court on King Street in Down Town Kingston. His supporters showed no respect for the law, the country or Jamaicans at home and abroad. His release was greeted with lots of gun shots outside the court house. The whole world was watching, and by showing disregard for the law, he paid dearly with his life. Spanner said "I didn't approve of the gunmen firing shots outside the court, in celebration of Jim Brown's freedom. I can guarantee that he will face a wicked death for shaming the country and the Prime Minister and it did happen".

It wasn't long before Jim Brown was back in GP again and this time he was facing extradition to America. He spent a good time at the General Penitentiary on F-Wing. Spanner said: "I remember one day, Jim Brown was going on a visit and he went over to C-Wing to check some of his foot soldiers and one of his ex-soldiers named Shatty Joe fist him in his mouth. He was the biggest don in Jamaica but Shatty Joe wasn't afraid of him so he disrespected the don. The don was upset with Joe and Chris (Chris was one of Joes partners in crime on the outside who he linked up with again on the inside), because they ran away from Garden to Jungle where they called themselves 'Cats.' Anyway, Joe hit the big man in his mouth and called him a 'batty boy' and he had to love it. Many prisoners including wardens wanted to kill Joe for disrespecting the big man but Jim Brown told them to let it rest".

Because of what he had done and allowed his friends to do outside the courthouse, he paid with his life. Jim Brown didn't get the chance to be free from prison that time, instead, he died in a fire in his cell on F-Wing and that was the end of him. Spanner said "It didn't surprise me to see him get murdered in prison by the state."

Zekes was another so-called don who dragged Jamaica's name in the gutter. There was that time when people were demonstrating for his release after they rioted and closed down, downtown Kingston. The whole world could see him at Central police station, waving his hands through the window on national television and telling his supporters to stop demonstrating and go home. The people obeyed his command and stop demonstrating and went home. Something would have to be done to get this guy, but the state couldn't kill him after he was released, because it would be obvious. They knew that he would eventually slip up, so the government waited until they got him where they wanted him. Zekes was supposed to die like Jim Brown, but somehow he was lucky to get a long prison sentence. No one should be allowed to disrespect Jamaica and live to tell the tale. This also goes for the police and politicians who constantly dragged the country to shame. Look at Adams who killed those eleven innocent people and got away with it?

Dudus was the latest don to enter the list of Jamaica's most wanted, but after one month he gave himself up. Of all the dons to grace Jamaica's shore, Dudus cost taxpayers the most money to repair the country's image. Reverent Miller a man of God saw it fit to intervene so that Dudus life could be spared. There is no doubt that the security force was out to kill him, but God inspired the reverent Al Miller to work as a go- between for Dudus and the government. For the second time in a decade, the State and its security force invaded Tivoli Garden and in the end 73 innocent people died. In 2001, the security force also murdered a further 27 innocent people in Tivoli Garden. In 2001 invasion of Tivoli Garden, Adams was the aggressor working on behalf of the State. He provoked the four days of killing spree that left 27 people dead.

Mr Miller knew that if the police did catch Dudus they would kill him, so he did the right thing by offering to help. Dudus didn't trust the police or his Member of Parliament, so he kept in touch with the Reverend which was a wise thing to do. If Mr Miller wasn't with Dudus they would have killed him. Not many politicians were happy that he was still alive because they wanted him dead, he knew too much and many businessmen who also helped him to get contracts and set up businesses are trembling in their boots. If Dudus decided to call names, it would be the biggest scandal Jamaica ever saw. There are too much at stake it seems, therefore, it would be better he was dead, than alive and free to tell the tale. Who gave Dudus the contract with UDC, and to fix mother White gully? It has to be Coke contacts in the JLP and people in the private sector who gave him work to do.

WILMOT MUTTY PERKINS

Spanner said "maybe I should contact Wilmot Perkins to get to the bottom of who gave Dudus all his contracts?" Mutty is good at finding out the truth and Jamaica needs more talk show host like him. Good work Mutty yuh large a foreign. People the world over listen to your radio program.

Corrupt Police and Public Officials

The Guanaboa Vale police, along with some from Kingston and Spanish Town and other gangs, were out to get Spanner and he knew that if they caught him, he would be killed so he kept on moving from one place to another until he migrated to the UK in 2001. People still are sending death threats on Spanner life even though he wasn't in Jamaica anymore, his family's lives were in constant danger. Spanner had too much information on corrupt politicians and public officials that could expose them, and because of that, many people wanted to get him killed because they feared exposure.

Take for instance 'Delano Franklyn' visit to Kitson Town, on his campaign against Mrs Simpson for the leadership of the PNP, and Alethia Barker distributing tons of rotten chicken back to the poor in West Central St, Catherine, for buying their vote!" Mr Franklyn can't say that I was lying because he spoke to me at the gate of Kitson Town Basic School, on the hill going up toward the Kitson Town Primary school where Barker was having a constituency meeting. We also spoke in St Mary at Camp Cape Clare in 1994; I also spoke with him many times after that while he was deputy foreign minister in the Prime Minister office.

Spanner had to run away and keep moving around the country to be safe from the people who wanted to kill him. There were police and gunmen in Jamaica who would stop at nothing until they got him killed. He knew too much, and he wasn't the kind of person who could be pushed around. There was a particular policeman who used to work at the Guanaboa Vale police station and who used to guard a former Prime Minister. Spanner gave this cop a gun to hand in to the relevant authority, but to his surprise, the cop gave the gun to a don who was guarding his crack house in Kingston 11, opposite the Olympic Garden police station. Spanner wasn't happy with the action of the cop and he threatened to report the cop to the commissioner of police.

The cop's response was to promise one day to get Spanner killed. It wasn't long after that, that the Guanaboa Vale police beat up Spanner and detained him on a trumped up charge of attempted murder. That was in August 2001, and they locked him up at the Spanish Town jail, with 18 prisoners in one small room. It took Spanner's family two weeks to get him out of jail, because of the charge they detained him under, and the arresting officers were cutting corners and using delaying tactics to keep him in jail because they were paid to do it. Spanner's aunt had to employ a lawyer to pressure the police and eventually they charged him for felonious wounding (GBH), he went to court and was given JA$30.000 bail bond.

Spanner's uncle bailed him, because there was a rumour going around that someone had paid for him to be killed inside the jail. Spanner saw many contract killings while he was in GP prison, without anyone ever being charged or getting extra time for their crime. He had to get out and he did, and two months later he ran away to the UK. There were cops, politicians and gangs out to kill him so he had to migrate. After Spanner got out, the Guanaboa Vale police was furious because their plan was for him to die inside his cell. Because he wasn't kill, that was when they stepped up the pressure to intimidate Spanner after he was freed, so that he would do something foolish so that they could have a good excuse to kill him.

The police would sometimes stop at Spanner's gate and pick trouble because they knew that he wasn't afraid of them and they could have some justification in killing him. Spanner ran the cops away from his gate one day, and a few days later, he got summons to attend court for indecent language. In other words, Spanner was charged for telling the cops to fuck off. In court, the Justice of Peace and the whole court system was on the side of the police. There was nothing Spanner could say to the court that they would believe, so he was fined $4.500 or three months in prison. He paid the fine but the pressure still continued.

It still didn't stop there, Spanner was up before the RM court on the GBH charge in a few weeks, and while in court the judge was like an evil witch. Spanner was dressed in this yellow linen suit with gold trimmings; the shirt was long and shouldn't be worn inside the trousers. On entering the courtroom, the judge said to Spanner "where are you going?" Spanner replied by saying "to court of course!" the judge replied: "if you put your foot any further, I will charge you for contempt of court" so, Spanner walked back out of the courtroom and had to tuck his shirt in his trousers before he returned to the courtroom. The judge was out to get Spanner and there was nothing he could say without the judge butting in and telling him to save his breath. He was still threatened with contempt of court and prison on many occasions.

Don of Dons

April-May in Jamaica is always mango season and that was when the rural communities of Kitson Town, Old Road, Pryce Pen, Top Mountain, Cherry, Dover, Banana Hole, Dark Hole, Paul Mountain, Kingsland and it's environ enjoy eating and selling their fruits. It was on a Friday morning back in the 1970s about 3:30 am in the morning Trinity journey to fame begin. The place was pitch black with lots of fireflies flying around show casing their beautiful lights; it was at that time the bus left Kitson Town, every morning toward Old Road and then proceeding to Kingston. The bus was old but reliable and always ran on time. Spanner remembered his grandmother would always wake him up to accompanied and help her with her load of baskets containing mangoes, nas-berries, cashews, sweetsop, sour sop and jackfruits, to the gate where the bus would pick up the goods. Sometimes the load would include guinnep, star-Apple, lime, bananas, yam, beans, ackee and sweet potatoes. In the evening, after school, Spanner and Busta would go and gather the mangoes so that his grand ma could sell the fruit in Spanish Town market.

Before Sylvan aka Spanner's grandmother left for Kingston she would always say: "Sylvan you must behave yourself until I return" Sylvan would reply: "yes granny, I will" and Dah would reply: "don't let me hear that you go to the river, ok?" The morning was cold, and Spanner was trembling. Busta was Sylvan's dog and he was always there to keep their company as usual. They could hear the horn of the bus from miles. Spanner lived in Old Road District which was a mile from Kitson Town High Street where the bus parked and quarter mile from where Trinity's grandmother lived. As usual, Busta got excited and started barking while running up and down the red dusty path. Grand ma would tell the dog to shut up and he would look up at Spanner and bark twice, and then start to wiggle his tail. It was Busta's way of telling Dah that he misses her and she should bring back something from the market for him. Busta was a member of the family and he was treated as such. He would guard the house and see to it that no one entered the yard without permission.

Busta was very useful, and one of his main duties was to pick up the eggs when the chickens laid them. The yard was huge, with lots of fruit trees and coffee trees, and the fowls would roam around scratching for worms and eating ripe fruits. The hens would lay their eggs in the bushes and the dog would go and pick them up and take them to someone. He was Spanner's pet, but he was grateful to 'Dah' who brought him from Kingston as a puppy. Dah was Spanner's and Pepper Pipe's grandmother. She was a short old lady with a welcoming personality. Spanner, his grandmother, Pepper Pipe and Busta were at the gate waiting on the bus which took about twenty minutes to reach them. The bus came and stopped by the gate to pick up Pepper and Dah with her load. While the bus was loading Spanner entered the bus as usual. He was a boy who had manners but he wasn't the type who took foolishness just like Errol aka Trinity.

While on the bus he told everyone good morning, while checking out who was on it. If he didn't say hello to the passengers, and his granny found out, she would be very upset when she got back from Kingston. News travelled fast and someone on the bus would be bound to tell Dah that Spanner didn't have any manners. So he knew he had to say good morning or (how-di-do) hello! On the bus he noticed that there were more passengers on it than usual for a Friday morning. In Jamaica, the rural people noticed everything, and if a stranger was in town everyone would know. That was how the country area ran. There were eight of his cousins friends on the bus and Pepper Pipe was joining them also.

There were people on the bus who loved Spanner and they promised to bring him back something from town for his good behaviour. He would always receive two Tastee's Beef Patties every Friday evening. The driver sounded his horn, indicating that it was time to move on. Dah entered the bus after seeing that her load was safely on the bus.

Mummy B, Errol's grandmother was also travelling on the same bus. Spanner got off the bus; the driver sounded his horn again in readiness, and then drove off with everyone waving to Spanner. He patted Busta on his head who was very excited and jumping up in the air and barking after the moving bus which left a cloud of red dust behind it. All the communities in and around Kitson Town was called 'Red Hills' because the dirt was red and looking like bauxite Earth.

In Old Road District the roads were very bad with lots of pot holes and had no asphalt on them, when it rained the roads became muddy and when it was dry the roads became dusty and all the trees by the roadside leaves would be covered with red dust. That was country life and life goes on along with poor management from the politicians that came with it. Sometimes people from many different communities had to block the main road at Kitson Town and Guanaboa Vale to put their voices across to the politicians who always made promises and never fulfilled them. Of course all those demonstrations fell on deaf ears because politicians only made promises and never fulfilled them. The bus was moving, and Spanner and Busta didn't move until it was out of their sight.

Busta was a brown dog with a short tail and big ears but very aggressive toward strangers. Spanner lighted his bottle torch (lamp) and along with Busta he made his way back to the house which was some distance away. Spanner was afraid of ghosts and that was why his grandmother bought him Busta to keep his company. There was no electricity in the community and it was very dark at night and all one could see in the bushes were Peanie-wallies (Fireflies) flying around shining their beautiful lights, gosh! The scene was amazing. In those days bottle torch was the order of the day. It was 5 am in the morning when Spanner and Busta reached home and Spanner went back to bed.

Fireflies were everywhere, helping to provide some light which was a beauty to behold. The Toads, Crickets and Birds were all making noises in the bushes, while Spanner was making his way quickly to reach home. On his way home he heard a noise in the bushes, which he thought, was a ghost, so he ran as fast as he could to get home. Spanner was a little boy of about 12 or 13 years but he was his granny's right hand. His grandmother loved him and only called him by his name 'Sylvan' and some people would say that she spoiled him and he was rude. Not many people liked Spanner when he was growing up because he wasn't someone they could push around. He wasn't afraid of anyone and he could defend himself even though he was small. Spanner was a slim boy growing up but he was fast on his feet and always likes to run.

Spanner's aunt (Miss Clara) lived at the same house with her husband and son. She looked after Spanner when her mother was not around; she was the one who woke Spanner up two hours later for school. Children in the country were used to that kind of life and they knew their duty to help around the yard. Kids sweep the yard, wash the dishes, picked the fruits for market and looked after the animals. Spanner had his breakfast which comprised of two boiled eggs, fried plantain and roasted breadfruit with chocolate tea before he went to school. Spanner was very good at athletics and his school always depended on him to win them medals. On that morning it was sport training day at his school and he had to represent his house, which was called 'Garvey House'. He went on a few weeks later to win the 100, 200 metre races, the long jump and high jump competition for his group.

The nine guys who were on the bus for Kingston to look for work, were Ramba, Errol aka Trinity, Pepper Pipe, Bernel, Luther, Gur, Maspan, Fishes and Marvin. Spanner, Regan, Maddo and Bummy were understudy to Trinity. The nine men would returned from Kingston the Friday night successful in their pursuit for jobs. They returned to Kingston the following Monday when they started their work. Nothing was heard from the men for two weeks. There were rumours going around while the men were away. It was rumoured that while the men were in Kingston on the Friday looking for a job two of them got lost!

Seven out of the nine men had never been to Kingston before that Friday. And to add insult to injury two of them did get lost! Trinity and Luther were the culprits and it would work out in the long run that the two of them would end up living in Kingston. The two guys that were lost were handed over to the country folks who sold their goods in Coronation Market in Down Town Kingston. That was how the story got leaked out about Trinity and Luther getting lost. Trinity's brother Bah got lost the first time his granny took him to down Town Kingston at the Coronation Market also but that was on a different occasion.

He was curious so he had a look around Spanish Town Road and got lost on one of the back street in Rema (a part of Trench Town where Bob Marley used to live.) Bah now resides in the United States but still controls most of Trinity's businesses. During the lost and found situation, Trinity made contact with some youths in the area where he would start work in Kingston. He was a clever dude and he made friends so that he could link up with them once he started working, and it worked because after a week on the work site he went to look for his friends and he never returned back to his job.

A few weeks later when he finally returned, it wasn't as a worker, but as a visitor to the construction site. Trinity wasn't interested in work anymore, but he decided to use the work site as a launching pad to enter 'badness'. Whilst all this was going on his grandmother was very worried about him. She didn't want Errol to leave, but things were getting from bad to worse with the cops wanting to kill him. She couldn't take the police visiting her home asking for her grandson every time and she didn't want them to kill him so she was happy when Errol left for Kingston to work. From the day Trinity left Crusher Construction site, he never worked again.

Once he used to work as a labourer but not anymore! It took months for Trinity to return to his community in Corner Lane near Kitson Town, but every month he would visit his friends at the work site. Every fortnight the guys would return to Old Road District with news about Trinity's progress in Kingston. He would bring stuff for his friends and told them stories about things he had done over the months: shoot out's with the cops was his favourite past time. He was also a good getaway driver too! He used to love watching western movies and he hated the ones where the marshals or sheriff killed the bad guys. Trinity was slim, light skin, about six foot tall, handsome, like to smile and always immaculately dress.

He used to celebrate whenever a cop got killed by a bad boy especially when Shabba and Copper were running things. His favourite song was Bob Marley 'I Shot the Sheriff.' Trinity always asked: "why didn't the gunman kill the sheriff deputy too?" Billy the Kid and Jessie James were like role models to Trinity. He always dressed like El Feigo Baka the Western character and that's how he got that name. Trinity's friends and family always asked him why he didn't return home, but there was nothing his friends or anyone could do or say to convince him to Kitson Town. He was in Kingston studying his craft that would one day turn him into a multi-millionaire and a legend. Spanner said "I can remember one day when I was about nine years old and police came from Kingston and Spanish Town looking for Trinity to kill him.

He was wanted for a murder and stolen cars, and the cops wanted him dead or alive; everyone knew that if they did catch him they would kill him. There was this old lady by the name of Ms Beth who loved Trinity and would do anything in her power to save his life. She was sick and couldn't walk too far, but after seeing the cops hiding and running passed her yard she had to do something to help. They wanted to ambush Trinity so she decided to do something about it".

Trinity-Errol was at Spanner's grandmother house where he and Pepper Pipe were cooking Ackee with salt- fish and dumpling. Only Ms Beth knew where to find Trinity and she wasn't going to trust anyone with that information. So she set off on her journey which was about one mile by road but half mile through the short cut, through Booth Town from her house. After doing half of the journey she got tired and her feet were hurting. She sat for a few minutes, and then she started crawling on her bottom for the rest of the journey. She found Trinity and Pepper Pipe at Spanner's granny's house and she gave them the news so that they could make their escape before the cops found them. By this time the cops were hot on their heels.

They reached the house a few minutes after the guys had left so they searched the house and found a 'Walter PPK' pistol. That gun was special to Trinity because it was the same type of gun James Bond used in his movies. In those days Trinity used to call those movies secret agent and the guys would use the movies for training purposes, which would include robbing banks and pay rolls from big companies all over Kingston. It wasn't long before a cop saw the back of Peppers shirt and they found out that Trinity and Pepper had escaped from through the back of the house. The cops started to spread out all over the place to see if they could use a short cut to head them off. They were like a hive of bees descending down on Spanner's granny's yard.

Trinity and Pepper were too fast for the cops and they got away. The first cop who reached the house stated that he saw when the guys ran off but there was nothing he could do. The cops were surprised to see the old lady at the house drinking a glass of cool lemon aid, and it took them awhile to figure out that it was Miss Beth who had alerted the guys. She was too old so the cops didn't bother to charge her for obstructing justice. They chased after the guys for the whole day without any success. When the day was over and night was approaching the whole place smelled of gunpowder and the police had nothing to show for their day's work. It was a joke for the whole community of Old Road, Pryce Pen, Corner Lane, Top Mountain, Old Road Bottom, Banana Hole, Dark Hole, Guanaboa Vale, Grant Town, Cottage, Content, King Land, Dover, Cherry, Fletchers and Kitson Town. Some of the cops were bitten by wasps, and some were bitten after running through a bee hive on Spanner's granny land.

Some got cuts from Kasha Macca (thorn) and one cop dropped into a pit latrine and was covered with shit while running through Gurr's father's back yard! There wasn't any pipe water in the community in those days so they had to call the fire brigade and use the fire truck to wash the shit off the policeman. It was a joke to the rest of cops to see their buddy covered in human excrement. There was this other cop with his eyes swollen and couldn't see because he had been bitten all over his body by wasps while chasing Trinity and Pepper. Busta was watching when the cops arrived and he barked as loud as he could to alert the guys even though he didn't like Trinity.

Busta was a sensible and cunning dog and he didn't want the cops to catch Trinity although he had bitten him before one night on his bottom. Before the incident happened, that day Trinity fed Busta, so maybe that was why he alerted him and it was a way of saying thank you for the food. Busta was like a soldier, defending his territory very aggressively and he ended up biting two cops. One of the cops wanted to shoot Busta but his superior, an inspector, came up just in time and asked the policeman "what the hell are you doing?" Trinity and Pepper were fast and they out ran the cops through the bushes.

After the day was over they sat under a number eleven mango tree and ate as many mangoes to get back their energy. The guys made jokes about how they ran the whole day and ran out the food in their belly. They ate mangoes and slept until the whole thing was over then they returned back to the community. The cops wanted to kill Trinity and maybe Pepper too who would have been a witness. Jamaican cops didn't like witnesses so they often killed them so that no one could give evidence on them in court. No wonder gunmen have to kill them so often and take away their guns. Trinity and Spanner were not friends of the police because the cops were always out to get them.

Muscle contractions were killing the guys after running all day from the cops and they could hardly move. Hence, they ate mangoes and slept. It was a good thing that they had had something to eat earlier before the cop's raid or else they would be hungry and dying of thirst. When the drama was over they were like lambs to the slaughter, they couldn't move after they returned to the community. It was kept as a secret about their whereabouts because of fear that the cops could return and find them in that state and kill them. People were saying that Trinity and Pepper had run out of steam. It was a joke all over the community that the guys were known.

Spanner grew up living in a close knit family with his granny, Auntie Clara, two girl cousins, Alicia and Mary and his aunt's husband's son, Omar. Later on, another granddaughter joined the family named Martha! Kitson Town was about 8 or 9 miles out of Spanish Town but the community was about fifty times the size of Spanish Town, which is the capital of Saint Catherine. (Spanish Town was once the capital of Jamaica when Spain ruled it but the British snatched it away from the Spanish in 1655.) Hence Jamaica was ruled by the British until 1962.

Spanner "the Arawak Museum is a stark reminder of how brutal the Europeans were to the islands first inhabitants." Spanner's grandmother lived on a big plot of land in Old Road District, thirteen acres to be exact, with all the fruits trees that you can think of. The land was self sufficient and Dah would sell the stuff that grew on the land to send Spanner to School, buy food and clothes and pay the taxes. Spanner was the apple of his grandmother eye and she spoiled him whenever she could and that makes lots of people envious of him. Trinity too was the apple of his granny's eye. With Spanner and Trinity there is lots of similarity.

The family were close, so there were other houses on the land. There was a one foot man called 'Jah' who was Spanner's cousin and the nephew of Spanner's granny. Jah lived next door to Spanner's granny's house and an uncle lived about three hundred metres away in a corner plot with his two sons Peter and Anthony. They were Spanner's best friends and they would visit their granny often because their father was close with his mother. His name was Uncle John and he was a barber who used to trim Spanner's hair for school. Auntie Clara was a dress maker and she use to sew shirts for Spanner's to wear to school. There was also another cousin and uncle who were close to the family. Uncle Liston and his son Michael, who we called Mitch, lived about half mile from where Spanner lived. Ralph was Dah's brother and he would sew Spanner's pants and school uniforms. His tailor shop was up by old Road top square beside aunt Teacia who was also Spanner cousin by his granny side of family. He was called 'Yankee'.

Uncle Liston had many fruits on his land also, and Dah, his mother was responsible for selling them. Spanner and Mitch would sometimes go to gather the fruits for market, but Brother Liston as he was called, was a very strict man and didn't like his son to mix with Spanner because to him, Spanner was a bad influence to his son. He loved his mother so he couldn't make it look like he didn't like Spanner. Brother Liston raised cows, goats, pigs and chickens and he also planted food stuff. Spanner's granny, Dah, was brother Liston's mother who also sold his food stuff at Spanish Town Market on a Saturday. He always supplied his mother with whatever food she needed. Spanner's dad wasn't around and after his grand dad Mass Gilbert also called Mass Gilly died, he started to get out of hand. He died when Spanner was seven or eight years old, and he was the only person along with his wife who loved Spanner like a son.

Trinity lived with his grandmother, two brothers, a sister, who later migrated to the UK and a girl that was adopted. The family attended church and Trinity's granny was a fruit vendor. Trinity didn't enjoy church, so he always made mischief. The four of them attended school, but Trinity wasn't keen to learn because he was always getting into mischief. He was his grandmother favourite grandson but he was always getting into trouble with the law. Trinity's grand mother's name was Mama. Trinity's name was Errol but his friends called him Trinity, or Elfeigo Baka (the cow boy character), while some called him Trinity or Errol. Mama, or granny, as she was called loved her Errol very much, he could do no wrong for her and whenever he got himself into any trouble she would bail him out.

He grew up on the wrong side of the law and ended up a career criminal in Jamaica and America. Trinity was a lovable and friendly young man, his grandmother thought so anyway. Mama and the people in the village called him Errol, but to his cronies he was Trinity. The heat was getting too hot for him because he'd got too violent and the cops were always after him. So he left his grand ma's house in the 1970s and he went to work in Kingston. While working on the construction site as a labourer with the others guys from his community in Kitson Town, he saw that working wasn't for him, so he left. From that day onward Trinity was destined to be a don in the criminal underworld.

He was delighted to leave the country area because the cops were after him and some of the citizens had begun to dislike him too. In Corner Lane, which is part of Old Road District where he used to live he wasn't well liked by the older Christian people there because he was a 'bad boy' to them. This gave him the determination to move from the area to Kingston where he could learn the craft of a real criminal. In every society there are people who like or dislike someone for whatever reason. Trinity's and Spanner were in that category, which was unfair on the guys because they weren't going around picking a fight or making unnecessary trouble.

While working in Kingston on Waltham Park Road (a very dangerous area in the ghetto), he met and lived with some real rude boys and gunmen, he soon stopped going to work. Trinity wasn't the type of bloke who liked work anyway so he turned to badness with his new friends. They called him 'country' until he earned their respect and became the respected Trinity. Those new friends were into all kinds of crimes and it suited him very well because he got the chance to become a shooter, gunman. While dealing in guns he also got the chance to specialise in stealing cars. That was an area where he was very successful and he really established himself in that field.

He was a specialist in the car stealing business and he earned a good living selling stolen cars. Trinity could now visit his grandmother in Kitson Town with his Kingston friends on a regular basic in all kinds of new model stolen cars. His action would cause lots of cops to visit the area again looking for him and his stolen cars. Sometimes he would take some of the cars to Kitson Town when he couldn't get the chance to sell the whole car; he would scrap them and then sell the parts. This guy was very good at what he did. He was a wanted man and all the cops wanted to kill him which would make life much easier for them. The cops knew that Trinity and his friends would steal a car every night and they were under pressure to catch him. So they would set up road block for him but he would shoot his way out and escape under some very skilful driving.

Sometimes the police would have shoot-outs with Trinity and even when they cordoned off the area they couldn't catch the guy because he was too slippery! He was loved by most of the young people who knew him and some would hide him until the area was safe and he was free to leave. The youths in the area loved to hear Trinity stories and they saw him as a Don and a role model. Most youths didn't like cops because of the way they treaded people by abusing their power all over Jamaica. Trinity had lots of friends in and around Kitson Town who he attended school with as a boy, and they worshipped him like a god.

There were also his friends who went to Kingston to work on the construction site with him, who loved and worshiped him and didn't want anything to happen to him. After he stopped working on the construction site he would visit the site to gossip with his friends about his life and time in Kingston as a Don-Gorgon. He was always a cheerful guy and his friends liked to be around him. To be in Trinity's company was a privilege. That was why Spanner would do anything to get in the company of Trinity when he was a boy. It wasn't hard though, because Pepper Pipe used to send Spanner with food or messages to Trinity.

Trinity spent many weekends in the country at his grandmother's home which was his head quarters when he was in Kitson Town. In Jamaica people called the mangoes that came from Kitson Town area 'red hills' mangoes because of the flavour and sweetness. There was a little hill behind his granny's house where everyone who visited him would stay, it was like a look out and they could see anything coming up or down Corner Lane. That is where Trinity would sit and tell his stories about his life in the city and how he shot after the police and ran from them after car chases. This would get Spanner excited and make him want to go and live in Kingston. In 1981 Spanner finally followed in Trinity's footsteps to live in Kingston permanently. One year later, he was in the General Penitentiary on a murder charge.

Trinity would tell the guys about how he and other bad boys had shot anyone who disrespected them and how he and his friends had even killed some of them. That was the way of life in Jamaica' ghettos and to some natives the ghettos were a no go area for them. Most killing in Jamaica is gang related but we must not forget that most people who got killed are mixed up in some wrong doing. Very rarely people get murder for no reason; there is no smoke without a fire?

Take for example someone visiting from a foreign country get murder in Jamaica. It could be that that person is visiting Jamaica and they put out a hit on his life. Many times a visiting Jamaican gets killed are because of their involvement and association with the wrong people.

Trinity left the area and no one saw him until a year later, then after that he started to visit on a monthly basis. He drove a nice car that he planned to sell to a man in Content District near Kitson Town. The man bought the car which was a Riley that was built by BMC in England. Two months later police took away the car because it was stolen. During that time Trinity would visit the area from Kingston driving flashy cars. He would drive a different car every time he visited Old Road. Sometimes the cars were so hot that he would have to park them in bushes and get them scrapped. He used to steal cars all over Jamaica from people who were rich.

That Riley car was the last car he would steal before he got caught and was sent to prison at the (General Penitentiary) in Kingston. That happened in 1977, and he was given two life sentences for all the crimes he committed over the years. All his family and friends were very sad and disappointed to hear what happened to Errol. His granny would visit him in prison for the next nine years. After all she was the only one who took care of Trinity from he was a baby and also loved him the most. When Trinity got into trouble with the law and got his two life sentences, Spanner was only fourteen years old, but he always keep abreast of what was going on.

Spanner used to see him when he came to visit his grandmother, although he wasn't in his league, sometimes he got the chance to sit amongst him and his friends. Of course Spanner would have to go to the shop for him and do what he asked of him. He would also visit Spanner's home to see his friend Pepper Pipe who was Spanner's cousin. He was Pepper's best friend and whenever he was in the area he would look him up. Trinity used to work on the same construction site and Pepper was the one who cooked the guy's lunch. He used to cook for Trinity because he couldn't cook.

Trinity would send Spanner to the shop and he would gladly go because it gave him the opportunity to get to know him and to be in his company. He would also give Spanner spending money from the change that was left. A few weeks before Trinity got caught the cops were hot in pursuit of him and they almost caught him because he was in a shop with his back to the police van that stopped in front of the shop. He couldn't see what was going on, but the shop keeper alerted him and Trinity just walked out through the back door of the shop. That was the nearest they came to catching him before he was caught. They were in Kitson Town looking for him and when they did glimpse him they chased and shot after him and Pepper for a whole day, but luckily they got away.

After doing nine years in the General Penitentiary in Jamaica, the notorious prison in Kingston, the Government reviewed all gun court cases and Errol's sentence was cut to fifteen years. He was released in 1986, on parole from the Gun Court at Up Park Camp. His friend, Donavan, another dangerous car thief, picked up Trinity at the Gun Court prison gate when he was released. Donovan was always in and out of prison, but he was a good friend and he respected Trinity who introduced him to the car stealing business. After a week on the street and free to do what he wanted Trinity and a friend by the name of Black Hat stored away on a banana boat from Kingston Wharf. They didn't know that the ship would stop off in Ochi Rios. They were on the ship for days before it left Kingston for New York.

The ship left for New York but stopped on its way in Ochi Rios, the guys were tired and they were asleep when the ship left Kingston. Black Hat woke up after hearing the ships horn, he looked through the window and saw the Jamaica Grande Hotels and other nice hotels and buildings on the North Coast and thought the ship had reached the State of Miami. He didn't wake Trinity up, so he made his way up the deck and then jumped off into the sea and start swimming toward the shore thinking that he had reached Miami or New York. Black Hat didn't have the decency to let Errol know what was going on, if he had, Errol would have told him that it was Ochi Rios and he wouldn't have to jump. If he had been to Ochi Rios before he would have known that he was in Saint Ann's Jamaica (his own country, for Christ sake) where Bob Marley and Marcus Garvey were born.

Saint Ann's is where Christopher Columbus landed when he claimed that he discovered Jamaica. It's also where Dunn's River Fall, Green Gratto Cave and the famous Fern Gully are found. Chukka Cove the world renowned polo club is also located in St Ann's between Runaway Bay and St Ann's Bay. Anyway, Black Hat swam to shore, thinking that he was in America, only to be greeted by fellow Jamaicans and the coast guard who detained him. Black Hat didn't get the chance to reach America that day, but the story about him jumping ship in 'Miami' spread everywhere, wherever there were Jamaicans. Trinity reached America a few days later and he never looked back from that day. He always talked about Black Hat's behaviour and he vowed never to help him after he became rich.

While in Jamaica General Penitentiary prison, Trinity used to sell cannabis like a drugs cartel or the mafia and he had staff and prisoners eating out his hands, he was destined to be a Don. Cocaine wasn't that popular in those days, prisoners smoked only weed. He was the Don of Dons and he literally ran the prison. He was well respected and there were many wardens' who brought the weed inside the prison for him. He made lots of money by controlling the drugs market from inside the prison. Trinity was so powerful that he could get anyone killed inside or outside the prison. There were wardens who would clean his shoes and kill for him because he gave and loan them money.

He used to loan the screws money because their pay were small change to what he was making inside the prison. He was so powerful inside the prison that every prisoner and warden had to respect him. He was like a god-father and most of all they called him the Don-Dada. He could get anyone killed or beaten up if they crossed his path but he wasn't a show off type of guy and he was very kind too. That was one of his many good qualities. That was why most people liked him because he was fair in his dealings; some even said he was a 'cool guy'. He was released on parole and within one week he was in America, after storing away on the banana boat from Kingston Jamaica, to New York.

It took him a week to get rich and within two weeks he was one of the most powerful drugs kingpins in the States. It was known in Jamaica that Trinity was the fastest man to leave prison and leaves Jamaica to America and get rich so quickly. He built an empire in the States and he helped many of his ex-con friends to get rich too. Trinity never sold less than one hundred kilos of cocaine. Anything below that amount, he would let one of his friend deals with it out of his supply of course. He was so rich that he owned one mile on two sides of the road in Miami of real estate. Trinity had many properties all over the States and he also built apartment complexes in America and Jamaica.

He ran other legitimate businesses too. Things were running smooth in the US until he ended up in prison again, this time he spend seven years in a federal prison. The Feds took away all his riches but he wasn't a fool. He came out and became even richer. His friends in Jamaica and America said that he was the luckiest man they ever knew. He went to Jamaica after cooling out from the Feds where he bought many more properties. This time he bought a 5, 000 acre property in the eastern part of Jamaica with lots of coconuts, mangoes and orange trees and lots of sea shore. He also bought a shopping complex in the uptown area of Kingston.

There was this shop in the community in Kitson Town where Trinity used to live before he went to Kingston that was run by a Butcher man called Toby. This shop served hundreds of citizens in and around the area. People from Spanish Town would come every Friday to Toby grocery shop to buy fresh beef and other meat. Spanner's granny's (Dah) used to cook beef soup every Friday for her beloved grandson Sylvan. Spanner was in his teens when the shop got robbed one night by gunmen.

While living in Kingston it was presumed that Trinity, with some of his friends came back and robbed the shop keeper. They took his gun and all the cash. Toby the owner of the grocery was a butcher also and he was the type of man who didn't bank his money. Toby was in hospital at the time of the robbery, and he had a heart attack and died when he heard about the robbery. After the robbery no one saw or heard from Trinity again until he was caught and tried at the famous Gun Court where he got two life sentences and was sent to GP prison to do his time.

Buckas, who was sleeping with one of the girls who worked in the grocery shop when the robbery took place, was beaten up and tied outside in the back yard, naked, syrup was poured all over his body. He was placed on an ants nest with the ants biting him as a punishment because Trinity as he stated, didn't want to kill him. When the police came ants were all over Buckas body and he was crying like a baby to be released so that he could wash off the syrup. The other occupants were left shaken up over the experience of getting robbed by gunmen. That was the first time I could ever record gunmen robbing someone in the community.

When Trinity returned back to Jamaica for the first time, one of the first things he did was to buy the property with the shop that people said he robbed. He tore down the old structure and he built a very big modern building with everything in it for his business and comfort. It was a nice two floor building and the upstairs was where he had his living quarters. On the ground floor, he had a shop, bar, wholesale and hardware store. There was this man called Precha who never liked Trinity as a boy growing up. He had three acres of land in front of Toby's shop where Trinity built his business place. Trinity tempted Precha with his money and he sold the land to him for a substantial sum. Not that it bothered Trinity because money wasn't an object, all he wanted was to own that piece of prime real estate. He had plans for Old Road, so he bought the land to build an apartment complex where all his rich friends could buy a flat and bring more money into the community.

This man Precha was the kind of person who wrote down all the kids' names who were born in the community and buried them under the big Cotton trees on his land. Precha was a man who dealt in voodoo. The first thing Trinity did was to pay some men to cut down the two cotton trees that towered over the community and blocking out the sunlight. Lots of things happened before the trees finally went down. A branch off one of the tree dropped on a tractor and killed its driver. The trees were huge and left the community looking dark no matter how much the sun was shining, Old Road was always looking dark. The cotton trees were blocking out the sunlight from the community while keeping the people down, so it was said by older people living in Old Road. After the trees were cut down the whole area lighted up and the district started to prosper again.

Precha's voodoo book was found under the cotton tree in one of its many dark crevices and was destroyed. From that day onward, his power was cut and he couldn't do anymore dirty work. Trinity bought every piece of land he could get his hands on in and around the area. He bought lots of vehicles to help with his businesses. He would also transport the old and young ladies with their mangoes to sell in Spanish Town or Kingston. One of his driver duties was to help the people transport as many mangoes as possible out for sale in town. That was a very kind gesture of him and the people loved him for it. He never collected any fares from the people he transported to sell their goods.

Trinity was a fancy dresser so too was Spanner but Trinity had the money to drive flashy cars and bikes. It was time for Trinity to return to the USA because he had accomplished most of what he wanted to do in Jamaica. It wasn't long after he left Jamaica that news came back to yard that he was back in prison. The FBI had been watching him and they caught him with half a container full of cash going towards the border of Mexico. He was charged with money laundering and murder and he was given fifteen years after making a deal with the Feds. He did seven years out of it, and was given parole. During the time he was in prison, his family and friends stole all that they could put their hands on in Jamaica. Some took cars, vans, bikes and cash. Before Trinity left, he told Spanner that he had over five hundred million in the banks that no one could touch and when he returned he was going to set him up. Spanner didn't want Errol to go back to America because he could feel that something was wrong but he couldn't stop him.

His grandmother died while he was in prison and she was buried without Errol attending the funeral. That was a big blow to him and it really upset him because she was all he had and cared about. When Mama was alive she used to take plane like taxi to the States compliments of her grandson. Errol would always send for her to visit him in the US. He bought a house for his grandmother in the States, where she would stay when she visited him. He didn't want anything to happen to her so he saw to it that she was safe. He would never let his granny stay at any of his houses because anything could happen. He didn't want to risk her health and safety because he loved her too much to put her life in any danger.

The businesses that Errol aka Trinity was in were very dangerous ones, so he couldn't take any chance with his Nan's life. He was a Mafia Boss for Christ sake, and someone was always out there to take a shot at him, or trying to take over the operation if he ever slipped up or got killed. Trinity was released from prison in 2000-2001 In America, and a week later he visited Jamaica after being away for eight years. This time, he was rotten rich and was known as the richest drugs Don from Jamaica. Trinity was much wiser, and he abandoned some of his first plans that he had before he left Jamaica back to America for a second time and he embarked on some new adventures. The property that he bought in Portland, the Eastern part of Jamaica, was a very strategic decision because it was to deal with his export business. He was in the process of building some private villas for the tourism industry in Portland. The Rio Grande River ran through his 5,000 acres property which was a popular attraction for the tourists who rafted down the Rio Grande River.

He got his export license to export fresh fruits to Europe and North America. Talking about Europe, his mom lived in the UK and became a citizen there when he was a baby. He never got on well with her because she didn't show him any love when he was growing up only his grandmother was there for him. After he got rich his mom started to show interest in him. So he went to the UK in 1987, and bought her a nice house in Chelsea. Errol was her favourite now, but he knew that she was a hypocrite because she never showed him any affection when he was a child growing up. Trinity was the type of guy who took care of everyone he loved and respected. His father didn't care for him either but he also bought him a house and set him up in a nice business in the States.

His father left Jamaica when Errol was a baby, for the UK in the late 1950s, but couldn't take the cold weather, so he left for America where he lived all his life. He did play his role in the end because he visited Trinity while he was in prison and helped took care of all his businesses until he was freed. Trinity's friends really liked him because he was a likable person and knew how to treat people. What he didn't know was that some of the people who his son called his friend were 'Wolves in Sheep clothing'. Some of them stole what they could while he was out of sight before his father took over. Everyone show Errol's father's love and respect because after all he was the father of the Don so they called him 'Dads'.

He came from America to Jamaica to look after Errol's businesses while he was doing time in federal prison in America, so he was now in charge. Spanner was working alongside Dads to see that things ran smoothly. Dads were in Jamaica for months at times taking care of his son businesses while Trinity was in prison. Trinity's dad was born in Old Road District and he inherited properties from his parents who had died long ago.

Trinity second return to Jamaica

After a few years, Trinity was back in town and people from all the areas that he used to live in while growing up in Jamaica were happy and celebrating his freedom. The people would come by his business place in Kitson Town to look for him and ask him for money. Everyone knew that once Trinity was back in town there would be lots of cash to give away and many people would get a job from him if they wanted to work.

He went to all the communities where he used to live and spent some time with the people there, sharing jokes and telling stories about his progress in America. Trinity would buy the food, liquor and share a couple of million amongst the people.

Within two weeks he gave away (16,000.000) to three communities that he once live. In Kitson Town where he was born and grew up he gave away ($6,500.000) in five days. Every person in the communities in and around Old Road District, who didn't care where he got his money from, was glad to take what he gave them. Every baby got a (JA$500) Nanny bill. People from Spanish Town came by van, car, bike and bus to collect their share of cash. It was like Christmas in summer (some people even joked by saying Santa Clause had come), in the rural village of Old Road District, Saint Catherine because of how the district was busy. People were happy for what was happening in Old Road once more and they were pleased how the place was busy again like in the olden days.

This guy was like Santa Clause! He gave Spanner ten grand in US dollars each time to get it changed into Jamaican money. His business place was as busy as a bank with the amount of cash that was around. Trinity gave away money that day until sweat was running off him like Dunn's River Fall. There were girls whose job it was to wipe sweat off Trinity. It was a sight to behold! While he was giving out money, a group of volunteers were cooking food for everyone and liquor was being distributed all around to whoever wanted it. He was like a modern day Robin Hood in the eyes of the people.

Money was no object to Trinity, because he had it in abundance and he also enjoyed every moment of it. After the celebration in his community was over, he went back to Kingston where he once live and continued to give away money to the poor. Trinity went to 77 Lane off Waltham Park Road where he once lived and there he gave away ($7, 000.000) to that community. That community is where he made his name in the badness business. He had many friends in that ghetto where he first went to work in Kingston. He felt he had to give the ghetto people money because they had taken care of him when he had just came from the country to live in the city. Furthermore, if he didn't give away money they could get him killed as a mark of disrespect. And they would say that he got rich and switch. Junior Reid, who was Spanner's friend and neighbour in Water House, sang about him not getting rich and switch, but many people do, and Trinity wasn't going to be one of them.

A few days later, he went to Spanish Town to the ghetto of Taws Pen where he once lived, and there he gave away $2,500.000. People from nearby ghettos included Ellerslie Pen, March Pen and Duncan Pen got money too.

At one stage of his life, he used to live in all three communities (Old Road, Taws Pen and 77 Lane) as a bad boy. Elfeigo Barka as he was called in the States was a famous and dangerous drugs Don in California, Miami, New York, Texas and many more States, and every drugs dealers knew and feared him. This guy got all his stuff from the Colombians by the trailer load and he sold his drugs at wholesale price. He was like a movie star and that was why they called him Efeigo Barka. Trinity was the type of person who did stuff that you would normally see in the movies. The things he did like changing car everyday of the week, was his way of playing a role like major stars in a movie. Lots of drugs dons in the States didn't like him because of his ability to make money and the fact that he was also a people person. Trinity didn't show off and was easy to talk to and very understanding, but don't cross him. Most of the dons were arrogant, cowardly bullies and repulsive with it.

Errol drove a dark blue Roll Royce fully equipped with all the mod cons. In that car he carried a gold attaché case full of (US$100) bill. Trinity would come out of his car and press his remote and the gold attaché case would just slide out from beneath the bottom of the car. Trinity wore £2,000 suits, snake skin shoes, Rolex watches and jewellery and he loved driving expensive cars. He fathered 22 children with eighteen different women and bought houses for all his kids' mothers. All his kids had (US$250,000) in their bank account. He bought friends houses, cars and started some off in their own legitimate businesses.

Trinity was untouchable in the States, he had lots of bodyguards and he was no angel. Word had it, that whenever he was in the States, he never trusted anyone. He was running a drugs empire selling hard drugs cheaply and that made him lots of enemies. So he couldn't afford to trust anyone apart from his family and close friends who helped him in business. He helped lots of people get rich and he also got lots of people killed. In the drugs business it was kill or be killed and in that kind of business it was only the fittest of the fittest who survived. He was ruthless in the States and many Dons feared him in America and Jamaica because he wasn't the type of person who people could play with or shove around.

Errol was kind and very understanding. One day in 1990, he was walking in down town Kingston when he saw an ex-con that he'd met while doing time in GP and he told Errol that he was hungry. Trinity gave the guy (JA$100.000) and told him to make himself a life with the money he gave him. Some called him the big man but he was a humble guy who had been through many situations, so he understood people problems (more than the politicians). He never excelled in school, but now that he was rich, it was his way of showing how successful he had become. While in prison in the States, he studied hard to catch up on his lost time at school, he wasn't any dunce, just a bad boy.

He turned out to be a shrewd business man in the end and everyone praised and admired him for it. He came from a poor background and he fought many battles to reach to the top. Errol had avoided death many times and had been to prison many times and his riches had been taken away from him three times by the US government. That didn't stop him from succeeding in life, because the guy was a fighter and he wasn't going to let anything stop him or get in his way. He even got a few DEA and FBI agents killed so that his business could go through. His riches gave him the fame and put him in a league by himself and that was what he always wanted since he was a boy. Trinity hated the FBI and DEA with a passion and he regarded those agents as pussies.

He liked to use a line out of DJ Super cat lyric when he was killing sound system back in Jamaica. It goes like this 'killing pussy and wi kill dem fi fun' Super cat was the roughest reggae DJ back in the days and he never leave his gun. He was also instrumental in telling DJ and reggae singers to insure their head because too many of them were being killed in questionable circumstances. .

Trinity wasn't a wanted man anymore like in the 1970s when he used to run up and down shooting people, stealing cars and hiding from the police in Jamaica. Now he could face the police and look into their eyes because he was rich, free and powerful, but not untouchable. Jamaica is a country with bad boys and dons who aren't afraid to kill anyone, some even specialised in killing police. It wasn't unusual to see a don funeral every other Sunday who got killed in foreign or Jamaica.

Foreign cops in Jamaica

The things that foreign cops do in their countries they couldn't try it in Jamaica because all a don needed to know is where that cop is staying and he was dead. No foreign cops could come to Jamaica and say he is a DEA, FBI, and Interpol or police because he would be killed like a dog on the streets. Remember that foreign cops put away lots of Jamaicans who have vowed to kill them if they ever put a foot on Jamaican soil. It was the disappearance of one of Spanner cousin from Kitson Town why the British cops were called in to Jamaica to help solve the case.

Spanner said "there are a few cops from the UK working in Jamaica and making trouble for the rude boys, but they have the backing from the government. What the government don't know is that these foreign cops will bad mouth them when they return to their country. They know that Jamaica's government and police are corrupt and they will let it be known to the media and Scotland Yard. These foreign agents don't like Jamaica or its people so they shouldn't be in Jamaica, period".

"There are some good police in Jamaica who could sort out whatever problems the country is having where crime is concerned if politicians leave the police to do their job without political interference. All Jamaica needs is to get rid of corrupt politicians, police, public officials and dons of course to free the country of crime. Not all police in Jamaica are involved in corruption and the good ones are tarnished by the bad cops. Spanner doesn't hate the police but he dislikes the way most of them behave by abusing their power, dealing in corruption and tarnishing the good men and women in the force."

Trinity was one of them who would kill foreign cops himself or order them to be killed like he had done in America and Jamaica many times. 'Trinity' was his alias and his favourite name in Jamaica, and this guy went through some real shit during his time in Kingston and America just to maintain his status as a Don. At one stage in his life while in the General Penitentiary in Kingston, he had to cut up a homosexual boy called Liam. In Jamaica homosexuality was not tolerated by anyone and you could be killed if you talk with one. In Jamaica, gays are killed, house burned down, and they can be cut up or stabbed to death.

Jamaica and Gays

Sometimes the same person who is doing the killing and stuff is also a closet gay too. Some even seek asylum in foreign because they are faggots and if they returned to Jamaica, they would be shot and their body dumped like rubbish. Some men who said that they were straight and killed gays are now some of the biggest gays in the UK and America today, that's a fact. Some of Jamaica's roughest and toughest gunmen were closet gays but they were Dons so no one could dare call them a batty boy or faggot because they would get you killed instantly. Trinity wasn't a gay, but he and some were friends because he done business with them. He wasn't the kind of person to judge people and people liked him for that. After the incident in GP where he cut up the batty boy they transferred him to the Gun Court Prison on South Camp Road.

That was where Trinity spent his last days in prison before he got paroled. He spent six months there among some of Jamaica's top criminals before he got his freedom. On the day of his released, his friend Donovan came with three cars filled with friends waiting to pick him up at Gun Court gate. Trinity came out of the prison holding one black plastic bag in his hand. Donavan was the only man in the group of friends that came to meet Trinity, all the others were women friends of Trinity and they would do anything for him. He had lots of girlfriends and many baby mothers who loved him to death. History has it that Trinity, Errol, Elfeigo Baka or whatever name he was called was the luckiest bad man to ever leave Jamaica's shore. He was the real big man where Jamaican don was concerned because he was running a successful drugs empire.

Trinity was a millionaire in less than a month, after he left prison and his home land Jamaica, for America. There were Jamaicans, Russians, and Americans who didn't like to see how he was running things, they were trying to kill him or set him up with the Feds, but he was always ahead of them. This kind of behaviour happened in every race and culture, there will always be Judas around. Someone who doesn't like to see success they always sold out people for whatever reason, sad, but true. A policeman said one day to Spanner, "We stick together" can you imagine if the criminals could do the same, we the police would all be out of a job?"

That same cop also told Spanner that he liked killing criminals and how he knew that one day he would not return home to his family alive. The same cop stated that he only needs to hear that someone was a gunman for him to kill that person and how he killed many people like that and put gun on them. Spanner said "while at InfoTech & Control working in the IT department one day I saw three guys brought in a computer to repair. They were boasting about how they hated thieves and gunmen. There was one in the group who looked like a rabbit. He was the one talking about the guy they killed and put a gun on him." Jamaican cops did that all the time to make it look like they killed a gunman. Sad but true, but the government turn a blind eye to it, and when a police got killed, as revenge, the whole country cry foul. If the government did root out that kind of behaviour from the police force, people would respect the police more".

The police reason for putting guns on so-called criminals, who they killed, was to protect them in court because the court wouldn't convict an officer of the law, who used his firearm to protect himself from being killed by a gunman. Spanner was disgusted with these criminal policemen! The policemen didn't know who he was and what he was capable of doing. Remember Spanner was in GP for murder and many of his friends were also murdered by the police. All the other guys in the IT Hardware department were surprised to hear the cops boasting about their crimes. Mr Baxter said "and come to think of it, when cops got killed people like myself are sorry for them and their family but not anymore" Lots of the guys hated the police from that day. The police have a long way to go if they want people to trust and confide in them. Most Jamaicans see police as corrupt criminals hiding behind their guns and uniforms.

For some people crime did pay. Take Trinity for example, because of crime he was wealthy and his wealth allowed him to rub shoulder to shoulder with the rich and powerful and it let him live in the same area with the Jamaican Prime Ministers and foreign diplomats. He used to live in one of his apartment complexes in Norbrook Estates, one of

St, Andrew's exclusive residential areas where all the rich people lives. That was where he lived when he was in Jamaica cooling out on the hills overlooking down on the city.

Trinity and Spanner journey to Kitson Town

Spanner said "I remembered coming from work one Wednesday evening when Trinity picked me up on Halfway Tree Road. He stops in the traffic and I hopped into his brand new 'Land Rover Discovery jeep'. As I got in the vehicle Trinity asked: Spanner what type of work your company do?" Spanner answered: "it's an IT company that does everything in computing" he said. Trinity replied "interesting, so what is your role or job?" Spanner said "I worked in the hardware department which comprises of building computers, computer lab, repairs and upgrading computers and laid cables. My department deals with banks, schools and all the Ministries". Trinity response was "so you're doing a very interesting job Spanner?" Spanner replied by saying "Yes, and I can let you meet my boss". Trinity grinned and said "'fantastic'."

They were now driving down Molynes Road approaching Washington Boulevard going toward Spanish Town. He told Spanner about his plans and what he had in store for him. It was the Wednesday evening and Spanner was walking toward Halfway Tree square to catch a bus that would take him to Spanish Town. While going across a stop light Spanner heard someone shouting out his name and a horn was blaring out loud. Spanner turned around and looked and he saw that it was Trinity and his brother in a Land Rover Discovery jeep. Spanner got in while it stopped in the traffic. There were people on their horns but Trinity didn't care, after Spanner got in he drove off and gave the others drivers his middle finger.

Spanner was taking home a tower computer with him so he was happy for the lift straight to his gate in Old Road District. Trinity's brother lived around 500 metres from where Spanner lived so they were neighbours. They talked while on their way to Kitson Town but Trinity didn't want his brother Button to hear some of what he had to say to Spanner. So he promised to meet up after Spanner had showered and eaten his dinner. Spanner did already told Trinity where he worked and he promised to stop by his work place the following day. Spanner told Trinity that he would be off work at 5pm which would be a good time for him to meet his boss. Trinity was bang on time the Thursday evening to discuss business with Spanners boss.

All the staffs were leaving when Errol stepped into the reception area. Spanner went into the office and told his boss that Mr Trinity was there to see him. The boss asked Spanner to show him to the office which he did. All three of them sat in the director's office where they discussed business. The boss wanted some cash injection into the company so Spanner introduced Trinity as an investor. They discussed business and shook hands on a deal. He told the boss goodbye and they left the boss in his office to prepare the document for the money that Trinity was putting in the business. Spanner was one of the boss's best workers and a personal friend, who saw that things ran smooth at the office when the boss wasn't around. Spanner and Trinity went down to the parking lot and sat in the jeep for about fifteen minutes while Trinity was making some important calls.

After he was finished talking on the phone, he drove out of the parking lot and headed toward down town Kingston. They went onto Ocean Boulevard to check one of Trinity's friends who was staying at the Oceania Hotel overlooking Kingston Harbour. The sight was beautiful and across the harbour was Port Royal. Port Royal was once known as the wickedest city on earth during the reign of Henry Morgan the Buccaneer. He and all the other Pirates, Black Beard and so forth were based there. They had a drink, then he and his friend chatted business. They didn't stay for long, so after Trinity was finished, he and Spanner went to the jeep and he drove off toward Kitson Town. It was during that time Trinity told Spanner about his plans, his businesses and where Spanner came into his plans.

One of Trinity and Spanner conversation before he died

Trinity said to Spanner "I am not surprise when gunmen shoot up the police stations and kill some of the criminal police". Spanner replied by saying "they did it at Browns Hall, Spanish Town in St, Catherine, and Olympic Garden in Kingston 11, Gold Street and Denham Town in West Kingston". " Trinity asked "and why is that?" Spanner answered "because the politicians and police were criminal. You and I know what those crooks are up to? They gives out guns to bad men in their constituencies to terrorise the people all in the name of winning their seat in parliament" Trinity "all those thing disgust me and that is the reason why I had to go to foreign to make some money so that I could help change people lives. There is always a way from letting those so-called leaders corrupting you. We both were corrupted by them but we saw what was going on and we backed out sooner rather than later".

Spanner asked "so why do you thing Jamaicans get such bad treatment from the US and UK, is it because we don't take talk from anyone?" Trinity replied "(wi likkle but wi tallawa) and can defend ourselves from any eventualities" Spanner "these foreign cops need to experience what the Jamaican police are going through and dem wi see dat (dem no fi mess wid wi). There are British cops working in Jamaica but it won't be long before some of them get kill" Spanner "did you hear what the youth said to the cops just then? He was swearing to murder a couple of the foreign cops" There was a silence in the air and it took some time before another conversation started. It was known that Jamaicans were being treated badly in foreign countries; they even referred to us as Yardy, shower Posse and all manner of bad names in the press especially in England and America.

Trinity said "It's not nice to see them working in our country knowing for a fact that they don't like Jamaicans, period. Spanner asked "did you know that the British and American government and public officials sees Jamaican politicians and police as corrupt? The court, police, Immigration and the politicians all see Jamaica's administrators and public officials as corrupt. Spanner said "I can't see why the Jamaica authority put out red carpet for these hypocrites when they visit our country and they don't like us" Trinity replied "to tell you the truth, I don't like those mother fuckers either, because they don't like us".

Spanner said "The British, Canadian, American and all the other countries who put out red carpet for the Jamaican PM and politicians are stupid also because they are helping to feed the corruption". They are adding fuel to the fire; these governments should demand accountability and good governance from the Jamaican politicians before they are allow setting foot in their country much less getting help. When Jamaican politicians get help from foreign governments, the politicians help their self first. That's double standard and the heights of hypocrisy".

Trinity replied "who cares? Spanner said "I noticed that when the

Jamaican prime minister visited the UK, I have never seen it in the mainstream papers or on TV that he is in town. They treat Jamaica with contempt and I don't like people disrespecting our country" Trinity said "let's change the subject because it makes me want to do something bad so let leave it at that" Spanner "ok" Ironically Jamaican gunmen and dons don't like or respect police, neither do they like politicians. They deal with the politicians and used them in the same way they used to be used by them.

He told Spanner that he liked the computer business and because of him he was going to invest in the company that he worked for. He told Spanner that he would be promoted in the company to a senior position to look after his interest. Trinity forget something at his apartment so he turned around and drove to his place on the hill in Norbrook, before he took Spanner to Kitson Town.

The view from the top of the hills looking down across the city was breathtaking and beautiful. They were at the apartment complex that Trinity built, up by Norbrook Estates, in the 1990s, after returning to the island for the first time. That was where he maintained his residency because he owned two of the 25 apartments, and sold the rest. Now that he was back in Jamaica, he was buying up all the available properties in and around the Norbrook area. Trinity was an ambitious man who took many chances and when he saw a good deal he went for it. He bought all the land he could get his hands on so he could develop them into whatever business he saw fit.

One of his latest business deals was buying a shopping complex in Half Way Tree. That he enjoyed because it was bringing him lots of cash in a short time. He didn't wear lots of jewellery like some Dons. He wore a gold watch, a ring and a necklace. The way Trinity dressed didn't really reflect his wealth, but when it came to money, he had plenty, and he had a good head for business. Trinity told Spanner about his many businesses and plans while driving down the hills toward Constant Spring Road, while taking Spanner to his home in Kitson Town.

He told Spanner that after dropping him off, he would have to stop at one of his work site to see what was going on. He dropped Spanner off at his gate and then drove off toward his business place in Old Road. Every day, he would visit his many work sites to see that things were going to plan. The workers loved him because he was a good boss who looked after them and he was the type of boss who ran jokes with his workers and sometimes he would buy the lunch. He could never be wrong for them so they always worked well.

Trinity was also a very good story teller and joker. Once he was telling some stories about past incidents involving him and some of his drugs friends in the States, about how he and some of his friends went to Mexico for a shipment of cocaine and it went wrong. Some of his friends got killed and when he was returning, his so-called friends robbed him of his consignment and left him in the desert to die.

He survived without food or water for days before he made it back to the border, where some people helped him. He hitched a ride back to the States where people thought that he was dead for days until he surprised all who robbed him and he had them killed. That was one of many tribulations he went through being a successful drugs dealer. Anyway, he was back in town again and this time it was different, because all who robbed him was dead and he got back all his money and drugs. This guy was clever and knew how to survive in a dog eat dog world. He used to drive tractor trailers from State to State and he had many connections. He told stories about how he would stay in the jungle for days while waiting on his goods to process (cocaine), amongst deadly insects, snakes and wild animals.

He told his friends what he went through because he didn't want them to believe that the drugs trade was a bed of roses or a nice game to be in, if you don't have the guts or stomach to back it up. Trinity said "Sometimes it was very hard to win but you have to just fight on like you're in any other business that you want to succeed in". Trinity told his friends that he didn't get his riches easy or by playing with people or sitting on his ass. There are lots of bad minded people who grudge him for what he had achieved, through blood and sacrifice. He was a supporter of the Jamaica Labour Party while living off Waltham Park Road, in Jamaica. Now that he was back in town as a very rich man, he was the envy of the People National Party and his so-called JLP supporters and so-called dons from both sides of the political fences.

Two of his closest friends who he left in charge of his business when he returned to the States robbed him of cash, a bike and a car. He just smiled and said that's life. Trinity also told Spanner that his so-called friends were foolish because they lost more than what they stole; they lost a good friend in him. He could have killed them himself or had them killed but he wasn't interested. His so-called girlfriend who was running the rental car business robbed him also of the company and over JA$40,000.000 that he gave her to bank for him in her name. Those are some of the things that happen when one is in the drugs business and laundering drugs money. One night Spanner and Trinity were driving past Suzie's house and Trinity said "Isn't that where that bitch lives?" Spanner replied by saying "yea" He just smiled and then changed the subject and they continued to drive in silence for awhile.

When Spanner was released from the General Penitentiary in 1990, after doing a stretch he was just in time to meet Trinity before he left the island for America. He was building his shopping complex in their boyhood community, so Spanner got to see him every day and sometime he would help Trinity transact his business in Kingston. Spanner went around with Trinity a few weeks before he went back to the States. Spanner also told him to cool off some more before he returned back to the USA which he didn't do. Anyway, they drove past the house and Trinity smiled like nothing had happened and then he said to Spanner "that girl was a fool because she could have had it all". Trinity wasn't an ungrateful person he remembered what she had done for him in the past when he was fresh from the country and suffering on the street of Kingston. She was his friend's girlfriend when he first came to Kingston from the country, and after awhile she started to like Trinity and over time it turned into romance. Suzie former boyfriend was Trinity's so-called friend, who had stolen his bike, car and cash. Trinity didn't date Suzie until after she ended the relationship with her boyfriend.

Glenville was the name they called the guy who stole Trinity's stuff. Suzie's dad had money in those days and was running a supermarket at the time of Trinity's plight. He was in the ghetto and had no money to buy food so Suzie would steal things out of the shop and gave it to Trinity. From those days Suzie had a crush on Trinity, and after a while they both ended up together. Trinity remembered where they were coming from so he left her alone. Killing her for the money she had stolen from him wasn't on his agenda. Trinity said to Spanner "the money Suzie stolen wasn't even half of what she deserved; because of greed she lost his friendship and trust".

After Trinity finished doing 15 years in a Federal prison, a small sentence for the crime he had committed, he was released again. He didn't tell Suzie that he was coming to Jamaica, because he didn't cared for her anymore, and it wasn't in his intention to hurt her either. That's the kind of guy Trinity was, if he loved and cared for someone there was nothing he wouldn't do for that person. However, if you also crossed him he could have you killed, just like that. After they drove past Suzie's house they went over to Portmore in Saint Catherine, (soon to become the 15th parishes) and Jamaica third City, where Trinity visited a home that he asked a friend to buy for him while he was in the States. The friend didn't know that he was in Jamaica and that he was coming to check out the papers for the house. This time Trinity was seeing to it that all his businesses was in good order and wasn't going to allow what happen to him the first time round happened again.

He was more careful this time with his business transactions. Spanner gave an account of what happen next "we reached the address and he stopped a few metres from the gate and Trinity walked up to the front and knocked on the door". A voice from inside the house asked: "who is that"? Trinity said "it's me man, open the door" The door opened and Peggy was very surprised to see that it was Trinity. She hugged him and invited him inside the house where they chatted and sorted out the papers for the house that he asked her to buy for him. Spanner and Button were left in the jeep outside for over two hours before Trinity returned. While in the jeep waiting, Button said to Spanner "can I invite you to church on Sunday?" Spanner replied by saying "thanks for the offer but I have to do some work on a friend's PC, maybe I will take up your offer another time" Button was Trinity's brother and at one stage while Trinity was in prison he was running his businesses.

It was after he and his brother fell out over the way he mismanaged his money, Trinity handed over the running of his businesses to his father, but as brothers they got on well. Everything was ok with the house papers, so he returned to the vehicle and they drove to the country where Spanner and Button lived and reaching their home he let them out. He spent sometime in the area with his aunt who was keeping millions of dollars for him. This aunt was a pensioner who had returned to Jamaica from the UK. She was wealthy, so Trinity banked hundreds of millions in her name because no one would suspect her. In the end she ended up getting most of trinity's money. That was in September 2001, when everything was going well for Trinity; no one could have envisioned that something was to go terribly wrong a month later.

It was the weekend before they went to the North coast to do business and enjoyed themselves. Trinity promised to do the East coast next time which would be soon. He was making arrangements to put some men on the farm in Portland. He bought tractors and just about everything that was needed on the farm so that things could run smoothly. There were things on the wharf to be cleared that were needed on the farm. He was really busy and moving like the world was coming to an end. Little did he know what was going to happen to him! He was doing what he did best by cheering up people and tying up his business deals.

There were people in the States running his businesses, legitimate business of course. His girlfriend parents were American and they ran real estate businesses all over the States. She introduced Trinity to her parents and they introduced him to the real estate business which he was delighted to learn about. He had the money to invest in real estate, so he welcomed their ideas with open arms. It interested him so much that he gladly took up the offer to run a real estate's business, a legal one. He bought many cheap properties and he made a killing out of it. His business was successful and he made millions from it. This success caused him to leave the drugs trade and stick to the real estates business while leaving his second in command to run the drugs.

Trinity was happy to find a business where he could wash his dirty money and turn it into legal cash. He was very good at negotiating and the change of business was good for him because he didn't have to keep looking over his shoulder for the Feds or other Dons who wanted to take over his drug empire. One thing he couldn't get rid of was the people who wanted to kill him and that he was aware of all the time. He knew that there were people who wanted to kill him but he didn't know when or where. This girl Tanya was a life saver for Errol; she loves him and wanted to have his children even though she knew that he had already fathered many. It would prove that Tanya was indeed the worst thing that could ever happen to him.

Tanya wanted Errol to marry her, but he wasn't into married life or settling down, not yet anyway. She changed his life, and turned him into a successful businessman in the States. He walked away from crime and was living a decent life now but there were men out there planning to (lick off his head) get him killed. Spanner told Trinity while they were driving through New Kingston one evening that he should set up a private security firm so that it could take care of his security needs, but he replied and said "God was his bodyguard".

He wasn't wrong, but he did need some men around him to defend him from people who wanted to kill him. The Bible says God helps those who help them self. Spanner told him that the firm could then guard him 24 hours a day. Trinity had been to prison so it would be hard for him to get a gun license to protect himself. Spanner knew that neither he nor Trinity could get a gun permit, so his plan was to get someone who didn't have a conviction to run the guard firm. Spanner would be the consultant and chief of security. This person who runs the guard firm would be able to employ decent and honest people who could get their gun licenses. Spanner would use eight of his most trusted employees; providing them with two Range Rover Jeeps that were bullet proof.

One of the vehicles would drive in front and the other behind with Trinity and Spanner in the middle. Spanner's plan was to get two or four corrupt cops in the group, so that they could kill first and ask questions later if anyone ever attacked them. When Jamaican police killed gunmen they don't get charged or go to prison and that was the end of the matter. Spanner knew that danger was out there and he wanted to eliminate it, before it happen but Trinity was moving carelessly. Maybe he thought that he was invincible, but not in Jamaica. He should have listened to Spanner who was more current on what was happening in Jamaica, Barrington Levy sang about 'going to Jamaica to catch the vibes', maybe he should have listened because if he did, it could teach him how to survive and save his live in the end.

Trinity said, "God was his bodyguard and he didn't need a gun". Those words were coming from a man who lived all his life not taking chances with his life and now he was talking like the 'Pope or Mother Teresa'. Spanner said: "maybe he should do a Ghandi." It seemed like he forgotten how much Jamaica had changed over the years. Spanner was a more modern street man who knew the running and was always on his guard for any eventualities. Trinity had change from bad to good, it seems and that have its implications. It's easier to get killed in Jamaica than say Iraq, Afghanistan, New York, Colombia or Albania. Spanner knew what could happen because he saw and lived it on the streets of Kingston, so he warned Trinity, but he didn't listen. He was encouraged to buy a gun for his protection and again he stated that God was his protector.

He wasn't interested in protection, whether by the law or by outlaws which he could easily get. There was always someone out there who would want to kill him he knew that, but he just didn't care. A rouge cop told Trinity that someone wanted to kill him and if he wanted his protection. Trinity turned down the offer because he wasn't interested. He wasn't worried at all because he knew that he could defend himself if he wanted to, so why worry? The cop was dirty anyhow and involved in drugs dealing and maybe he knew what was going on and tried to tell Trinity but he didn't listen. Spanner thought "maybe he was a part of the conspiracy"

That cop killed many gunmen and also protected many business people and Dons across the island. He was an official extortionist. Spanner told Trinity about an incident he saw while visiting friends in Ochi Rios. Spanner said, "I was in Ochi Rios and I saw a crowd and when I took a peep, I saw the same cop coming out of a notorious drug don business place. This cop Magul travelled all over Jamaica collecting extortion money from criminals and business people" Trinity replied and said, "but Spanner you know that, that's the game with Jamaican cops" Trinity was really trying to change his life so to hell with who wanted to kill him. When he was driving the Discovery Jeep, he was more on a low profile because no Dons drove that kind of vehicle in Jamaica.

The drugs Dons were all driving F150 pickup trucks so he went and bought a brand new white one to move around in and blend in with the crowd which was foolish of him. The F150 Truck was more acceptable in the Dons culture and it was the latest addition to his collection of vehicles. He did look more respectable in the Discovery because it was different and only rich business people in Jamaica drove Land Rovers. Trinity loved anything that was made in Great Britain. He didn't like living in the UK though because it was too slow for him but he spent time there when he visited his mom. He never lived or stayed in the UK for over a week but he had his British passport. How he got it was unknown but whatever Trinity wanted he got. Spanner said "the Queen is his nanny so it's no surprise he got his citizenship"

He was also a US citizen and a Jamaican at the same time. He was so rich that he got what he wanted like those guys in the CIA or mafia movies. He was real and not an actor but a Jamaican at his best. After he finished serving his sentence in the States they wanted to deport him to Jamaica but they couldn't because he was a British Citizen so they deported him to the UK. How he managed that God knows.

Trinity spent one week with family and friends before he returned back to the States. This guy was a genius and he had contacts in many countries. While in England he stayed in Brixton, Birmingham, Bristol and Manchester. Trinity had two of his baby's mom living in the UK, his mom, sisters, aunties, uncles and cousins all lived in the UK. He also had many friends who ran business in the UK on his behalf. Elfeigo Baka ran a global empire and the UK was one of his favourite places to do business because of the value of the pound and the price a kilo of cocaine cost there. He loved the UK and he even said that the Queen was his nanny.

He liked anything made in Great Britain but he claimed that England was too slow for his life style and that was why he didn't spend more time in Britain. He liked countries where he could carry a gun anytime wherever and whenever he chose. In Brixton, Birmingham, Bristol and Manchester he was a legend to the people from his community in Old Road District, and Jamaicans who knew him. Trinity wasn't a friend of Scotland Yard, MI5, MI6, or the CIA and FBI for that matter. He told Spanner that if it was in the States or Jamaica lots of agents would get gun down just for target practice. He told his friends that British cops were stupid and a joke. Trinity said, "They don't even carry a gun for Christ sake" He also reminded Spanner that it was the CIA and MI5 who killed Bob Marley. Spanner replied, "I know that blood, Bob Marley was too radical and he was wising up people all over the world about the capitalist dem, who happened to be Britain and America. So they joined together and killed him."

Trinity even made a serious but relevant joke about how Nanny the woman Maroon slave leader in Jamaica, beat the British who were a super power in those days at their own game. Spanner told Trinity about how Jamaicans were the first people to invent camouflage and also guerrilla warfare tactics to kill off the British. During the struggle the British soldiers would see the trees moving but didn't notice until it was too late. The slaves used the trees as disguises to attack and kill the soldiers. Nanny later became Jamaica only female national hero, her picture is on the JA$500 bill.

Trinity and Spanner visit to the North Coast

During Trinity's busy schedule he and Spanner visited some of Jamaica's most beautiful attractions and residential areas. The reason for that was because the guys loved their country and didn't like how Jamaica was being portrayed on foreign news media. They even talked about how tourists were enjoying the country more than people who born there. Not that it was a bad thing, because the country needed the money that these people spend. The guys loved to enjoy Jamaica's beautiful sceneries and all that it had to offer. They lamented about not being able to see Jamaica's beautiful houses, roads, beaches, mountains, various fruits and buildings on foreign televisions but only the bad bits. Spanner said "I would love to see the foreign press showcasing more positive thing about Jamaica. I guess they are more interested in the negative. What about all the rich foreign kids attending boarding school in Jamaica whose parents are diplomats and other high profile people? You don't hear or see that in the foreign news?" He asked.

The only time one ever saw Jamaica on television was when something bad happened in the ghettos which was not fair. The incident in Tivoli Garden in 2001 was all over the news and the foreign press. Spanner said "it's sad though how the government murders its citizens and nothing comes out of it. It was business as usual. The police and army lost that war but watch out because they are going to pay Tivoli another visit and this time there will be many more killings by the state."

The US is rich but if you have money in Jamaica like Trinity had it, you could be more relaxed and less stressed. Apart from the violence in a few garrison communities in Kingston, Spanish Town, St. James and Clarendon, life was nice in Jamaica. Crime is everywhere across the world, in the UK and US, some of the worst crimes committed, but you don't hear the news media saying don't go to those countries. What Spanner and Trinity wanted, was to launch an advertisement campaign to show how beautiful Jamaica was. Spanner was instrumental in implementing the creation of a Park and Farm in Old Road, even though he didn't get the credit for it. Lots of the hotels showcase sand and sea but Spanner and Trinity wanted to showcase the people and everything good that the country have to offer to the world.

If something serious happened in Jamaica you would surely hear the British Foreign Office and the US State Department advising their citizens not to visit Jamaica and all sorts of negativities. When Trinity, Spanner and their friends visited Ochi Rios and Montego Bay beach and all the other tourist attractions in Jamaica, all one could see were tourists enjoying themselves. Spanner asked "If Jamaica wasn't heaven on earth or paradise why would so many tourists leave their countries to visit Jamrock? Millions of tourists visited Jamaica every year, so the people and the country must be nice and safe if so many tourists continue visiting?" They went to Ochi Rios and Montego Bay to checkout some of Trinity's properties and others that he was buying.

On the day in question, the group left Kitson Town early in the morning at 5am and they reached Ochi Rios after 7am. They left Old Road District, via Kitson Town and turned right on the main road which took them through Guanaboa Vale. They took the shorter route through Guanaboa Vale, Store Hill, and Copper turn, Cujoe Hill - where the slaves used to store their money, through Back Pasture, Water Mount, Browns Town, Point Hill, Luidas Vale, Tydixon, and Clover Hill and eventually they dropped out at the Moneague Police station in Saint Ann's. They turned left and drove through Fern Gully into Ochi Rios.

While going to Ochi Rios they had to drove through lots of orange and sugar cane plantations on both sides of the road while approaching Luidas Vale where there was a sugar cane factory. They stopped to eat a few oranges, they were sweet and the trees were loaded with ripe fruits. On both sides of the road was Luidas Vale Estates with acres of orange trees laden with ripe fruits. It was only when they reached Tydixon, a farming community where lots of Spanner's friends lived, before they were in a proper little village. The drive was lonely but safe. They didn't pass much traffic on the country road, only a few sugar trucks taking sugar to the wharf in Ochi Rios to be shipped off oversees to America and Europe.

They had breakfast at a Rasta man cook shop which comprised of mint tea the Jamaica term for (bush tea) roast bread fruit with ackee and salt fish. After the group had finished having breakfast they had fruit juice to wash down the food. The fruit juice was comprised of pineapple, mango, orange, guava and banana blended up together with natural honey added. The breakfast and tropical punch was wicked (good). Lots of tourists were in line to get theirs and the ones before all enjoyed their drinks too. Some of the guys had cooked banana with ital strew that was the dread's special. Trinity and Spanner visited Dunn's River Fall where they spent hours enjoying one of Jamaica's most beautiful attractions. On the beach were lots of tourists enjoying themselves?

It was time to have lunch after they finished checking out some guest houses, a petrol station and a night club that Trinity had already bought. Most of the time was spent driving around looking on some other properties that Trinity wanted to invest his money in. Spanner commented to the group, "If my memory serves me right Christopher Columbus and his bunch of criminals were the first tourists to visit Jamaica in 1494 and to enjoy its beauty". It was lunch time, so Spanner and Trinity went to the cook shop where they ordered curry goat with white rice and two glasses of sour-sap juice.

The other guys had various other Jamaican dishes mainly consisting of dumpling, yam and curry chicken. They finished lunch in 20 minutes and then headed to Green Grotto Cave. This time they didn't have a swim, all they did was explore the cave and its natural environment. Time was running out so they promised to return another time and they then left. On their way back to Ochi Rios town they stopped on the wayside and bought two bottles of honey and two bottles of roots juice from a Dreadlocks. Trinity even bought some beautiful Jamaican crafts from the dread, to take back to the States for his kids. They didn't stop for long because they had more places to visit and some more properties for future purchases.

Spanner asked the driver to turn off the main road to Ochi onto Pimento Walk Road where The Shaw Park property was located. The Hotel was just a stone's throw from Ochi so there was no need to hurry. Five rooms were booked at Jamaica Grande Hotel in the heart of Ochi Rios. They continued up the road until they reached Pimento Walk where Spanner had many friends living and where he spent plenty of time before. Spanner's friend Satta John lived in the area where his family had lots of land, big mansions and businesses. Satta John's father ran a patty bakery (pastry) that supplied outlets in Ochi Rios. It wasn't a long visit, but everyone was glad to see Spanner and his friends. He couldn't visit Ochi without seeing his friends because that would have been criminal.

The guys were told that there would be a dance in the area and there would also be a beauty pageant taking place to choose Miss Ochi Rios.

Spanner and Trinity told Satta John that they would attend the dance but they couldn't stay out too late.

While in Ochi Rios, two British and American tourists got robbed at gun point by two men from Kingston. It seemed like they were new to the tourist town so they proceeded to rob the foreigners. Little did they know that it wasn't like Kingston and it was the worst crime a person could commit, by robbing the tourists? Justice was swift. The three ladies reported the incident to the cops who were quickly on the scene. They described the two guys who robbed them and the clothes they were wearing. The tourists returned to their hotel to await further news. While in the hotel bar at Jamaica Grande, Spanner was having a cold Red Stripe Beer while Trinity was having a Ting Grapefruit juice when two cops approached the bar. They didn't ask any questions but walked over to the three ladies in the corner at the table.

The cops joined the ladies and chatted for a few minutes. The ladies then finished their drinks, took up their belongings and walked out with the cops. Spanner asked the bar tender what was going on and he was told that the ladies were robbed earlier on. It was after the ladies returned that they knew what had just happened. They were told that the cop took the ladies to identify one of the robbers. He was killed 30 minutes after the robbery and the police took a 45 colt off him. His friends were in the hospital fighting for his life. In all, the cops got two guns that day from the robbers. The cops reassured the ladies that in Jamaica they dealt with justice swiftly. After the cops showed the ladies the dead body one of them fainted.

In the UK you would never see the cops kill someone and then witness be taken to identify the body on the street and not in a morgue. In Jamaica, it was different, because the cops were judges, jurors and executioners. The tourists were happy to get back their bags with their stuff but were sad on the waste of life. The other criminal was lucky because Jamaican police don't take in gunmen alive. There were lots of witnesses who saw what happened and they told the cops that they would report them if they killed the other one in cold blood.

That was why they didn't kill him on the spot and he was taken to the hospital. His luck didn't stay with him for long because by the next morning he succumbed to his wounds and died. In the hospitals the nurses and doctors don't like gunmen so they are not keen on going all out to save their lives. Lots of nurses and doctors got robbed by some of these so-called gunmen so they were not too sorry for gunmen when anything happened to them, when they ended up in hospital.

The guys were having a good time in Ochi Rios. When they reached the dance in Pimento Walk, the beauty pageant was over but the guys got the chance to see all the beautiful girls in their outfits with the company's names that sponsored them. Satta John introduced the ladies to Spanner and his entourage, one of the beauty pageants was Satta John's niece who already knew Spanner because he had spent plenty of time with her family in Pimento Walk. Spanner and his friends Sheriff and Brando used to spend weeks in Pimento Walk before the visit with Trinity.

Spanner ordered champagne for the ladies and they all took group photos. Spanner even got a few phone numbers. After partying for a few hours Trinity was ready to go into Ochi Rios to drive around to see how the town looked at 2am, in the morning before they went to bed. The night life was vibrant and lots of people were moving about their business. They drove into the hotel car parking lot 20 minutes to 3am. Trinity was the joke of the group because he had two ladies to go to bed with. They said good night and went to bed and the rest was history. It seems like Spanner didn't get much sleep because all through the morning you could heard rumbling in his room. It was like he was doing overtime. One of the guys' had to knock on his room wall and asked Spanner to cool down because he wanted to sleep.

Spanner was the first one to be up the next morning at 8am and he went and woke the rest of the guys. Trinity came out next and told the rest of guys to get ready in half an hour's time because they were all going to Montego Bay, but first they would stop off at Doctor Cave Beach, which is in the parish of St, James. They drove out of Jamaica Grande hotel car park at 9am and reached Montego Bay at 10.30 am. They didn't eat at the hotel but had tea before they left. Before leaving Ochi Rios they decided to visit Rose Hall Great house where the White Witch of Rose Hall once lived. It was one of Jamaica's famous attractions because of the tale behind the witch and all her lovers that she murdered.

It was believed that Rose Hall great house is haunted with the ghost of Annie Palmer. They stopped before reaching the great house to have breakfast. Spanner had cornmeal porridge, also fried dumpling with steamed callaloo with salt fish. Trinity had porridge, with bammy and fried fish. The rest of guys had cooked food: yam, green banana, dumpling with salt fish and okra. For drinks, they all had peanut punch. They all laughed and come to the conclusion that with all the workout the guys got especially Spanner, last night everyone needed the extra stuff hence they had some proper power juice. In Jamaica peanut punch juice is considered to be good for the libido. Spanner was a good cook and considered himself, a good food critic.

He would test the food and tell the chef where he/she had gone wrong, he would also be the first one to praise the chef if the food was good. This guy was a specialist on Jamaican dishes and natural juices and he could tell if foreign dishes were up to standard too, he had a clean palate. The best place to eat in Jamaica was not in hotels but at one of those cooks shops on the wayside or tucked away in the corner of nowhere. They toured the haunted house and Spanner claimed that he saw something move in one of the rooms. Everyone started to laugh because Spanner was always saying that he could see ghosts, but this time he was just taking the piss.

It was a curtain Spanner saw move and he thought it was Annie Palmer in her white negligee. He had the gall to say that the ghost looked sexy too! After the tour of the mansion, the group went down to Rose Hall beach. The beach was full of American, European, Canadian and Japanese tourists. The cruise ships were docked off the course not far from the beach. After walking around they saw that there were Chinese and Russian tourists on the beach sunning while some swam in the sea. Some were relaxing on the beach drinking rum punch and other Jamaican cocktail drinks.

Trinity was the first one to enter the water, then Spanner, who was familiar with the beach because it wasn't his first time there. Earlier that year Spanner and some of his friends from Kingston, who lived in the UK, visited the island and them and Spanner went to Doctor Cave Beach. Spanner knew his friends while living in Kingston in Water House when they used to roam the streets shooting at police and doing other wrongs. His friends visited him and brought him many gifts which included jewellery, expensive clothes, shoes, trainers and money.

Everyone went for a swim and didn't get out the water until 1.pm; the water was warm and very relaxing. It was lunch time so they returned to the same cook shop run by the dreadlocks where they had lunch. Before everyone had their lunch they were given a bowl each with fish soup (fish tea) it was very delicious and all enjoyed it. Spanner ordered turn cornmeal with steam doctor fish with okra and lots of vegetables. Before Spanner left the cook shop that morning he had told the Rastafarian what he wanted for his lunch.

Everyone had turn cornmeal with steam doctor fish with okra and plenty of steam vegetables. They all enjoyed the lunch and for the ladies from the States (Vicky, Tara, Samantha, Stephanie and Jodie) it was the first time they were eating that type of food. There was a discussion going on about how wicked the food tasted and the ladies were saying that they were going to cook it when they return to the United States. Spanner said "this food makes you strong enough to shag your woman long and it's better than Kentucky, Mac Donald's, Taco Del, Subway or Kenny Rogers".

After they finished having lunch Trinity took them to a (bureau de change) they thought he was going to change some money, but to their surprise he owned it. Spanner and Trinity went into the office to see the manager and Trinity introduced himself to him. They didn't stay long because Trinity made plans with the manager to return at a later date. They left the bureau de-change and headed toward Gloucester Avenue where he had an appointment with a night club owner. It wasn't long before they were in the heart of Montego Bay tourism business district, where all the hotels are located. The street and buildings were beautiful. Some of the guys couldn't believe how beautiful Jamaica was after stepping out of their comfort zone for the first time. Some of the guys compared Montego Bay to Miami and California.

It was their first time to the second city so their excitement was understandable. Spanner said to the guys "that's why some of you should leave your community and enjoy your beautiful country" Spanner had been to Montego Bay many times and he spend time in Salt Spring with his friends. They reached the night club and spent a good time in there, when they were about to leave, Trinity told the guys that the club belonged to him, Spanner already knew. The club was nice, and it looked like some, one would see in the movies. Rooms were booked at Rose Hall Hotel, so they weren't in any rush to get out of Jamaica's second city. Trinity had friends in Flankers and some of them had been in prison with him. There was one by the name of Devil who had just got out on parole after 25 years inside. Trinity couldn't visit Montego

Bay without checking Devil and his family after what he had done for him while they were in GP together. He was the one who used to store Trinity's drugs and knife and he was also one of his enforcers in the prison.

They went into the ghetto to look for some of his other friends because there were some who got out before Devil, who Trinity also wanted to see. When the vehicles entered the community lots of people were peeping over their zinc fences. While further down the lane a M16 rifle was pointing at us, and across the road another man pointed his pistol at the driver's head. It wasn't long before they heard a voice saying that everything was ok and the guns stopped pointing at us. Devil came over to the jeep and Trinity got out and the two men hugged while fists were being thumped all around. While all this was happening some kids were still playing on the street. Before they saw what was going on they stopped and asked the kids for Devil.

One of the kids did point to a board house over the other side of the road, the same place where Devil came from to greet Trinity. At Devil's gate two big dogs jumped at Spanner when he was standing too near. After the people saw that everything was ok they all came out to see what was going on. What Spanner and Trinity didn't know was that two nights before five people were killed because of gang violence. The place was hot like fire but Spanner and Trinity were not afraid of the ghettos because they grew up in some of Kingston worst areas for violence. After Devil was freed from prison he took over the area leader role as the new Don. They walked down the lane to the only concrete shop and ordered drinks for everyone including women and children. There were lots of people who came out of their yard and followed them to the shop. Trinity told Spanner to give the women and kids what they wanted. Some got money while some ordered baby food and just about every kind of grocery.

It was clear for everyone to see that poverty was rampant in the area. It was obvious that the politicians for the area weren't doing anything for the people of this particular community or for the constituencies. The visit was like Father Christmas appearing from nowhere. Some of the guys were standing guard with their M16 rifles while some had pistols as protection for Trinity and his group. The ladies didn't feel safe with so many guns around them but Trinity reassured them that everything was ok. Spanner paid the shop keeper (JA$45,000) for the goods that the people ordered. While another $10,000 was paid for the liquor and Trinity gave Devil (US$2,000) and told him to call him before he returned back to the United States.

They all said goodbye and drove out of Flankers at 7pm, and headed to the hotel where they had a shower. After the shower they went back down to the dread cook shop where they had dinner. Some of the guys had jerk chicken with festival, while Spanner and Trinity had roast fish with roast yellow yam. The cornmeal that they had for lunch earlier in the day was still in them so they didn't have a big dinner. They had Irish moss and some of the Rasta roots juice to wash down the food. As always they enjoyed the dread's cooking and Spanner rewarded the Rasta man handsomely by giving him three ($3,000) grand in Jamaica dollars as a tip. The dread was happy and told them to return another time.

Trinity had an appointment at Round Tree Hotel for 8:30pm so they drove over to the hotel to see his contact. He was dealing with a shipment of cocaine from Colombia to the US. Trinity went into his room and left Spanner and the rest of guys in the hotel bar. Half an hour later they saw Trinity returning back smiling and everyone all knew that a deal has just being closed. He was happy with his contact and the progress but to the guys surprise Trinity announced that he wouldn't be staying out late. He stated that he had to wake up early the next morning for Kingston where he had a two hundred and fifty room's hotel under construction in New Kingston.

They returned back to the hotel after they finished their day activities, Trinity was tired so he decided to cool out the night in his room with his two ladies friends Samantha and Stephanie. Spanner on the other hand was acting like he was Mr Lover, lover with his girl. He was happy to be able to spend another night with Vicky. Button was a Christian so he didn't get any of the girls. The driver love off Jodie and they get on like two teenagers falling in love. As for Tara she was really into Spanner cousin Chocolate who was a dread. She heard Chocolate sing and she fell in love with him. Tara even promise to marry her man and file for him to live with her in America. So far everything was working out well for the guys and the girls were up for another night of fun.

The guys spend an hour in the bar drinking before they went to their bedrooms. Spanner was the first one to left the bar for his room.

The night before he didn't have much sleep, because of his marathon love making. Everyone was surprise to see Spanner heading off to bed so early, so the guy had a bet on him doing another marathon with Vicky. Before Spanner left the bar he told the guys that he rather died making love to a woman than die alone. By 11.pm everyone was in their hotel rooms and they could hear Spanner still having a good time. Vicky was making lot of noise, maybe Spanner was working overtime. The next morning the guys were up very early for their journey back to Kitson Town.

It was time to go and Trinity told the drivers that they should take the South coast back to Kingston; he also told the guys that they would be having breakfast in Negril, where he had to make a stop to check on some properties that he bought in the West End. Spanner told the drivers to drive up to Red Ground where he had some friends, and that was where the group had their breakfast at Nia-bingy cook shop. There wasn't much time to spend in the area so the group had peanut porridge and banana fritters. After breakfast Trinity took the guys to see one of his properties which were a guest house with forty rooms and a marina. It was beautiful, and the sad part of it was that they couldn't stay to enjoy the facilities because time was running out on them. Trinity's lady friends had to return back to Ochi Rios where they were staying. They all said goodbye to the ladies even though Spanner didn't want his girl Vicky to go. The girls went north and they headed south. Driving back to Kingston on the south coast was a beautiful experience. Especially driving through Holland Bamboo Walk where bamboo grew on both side of the road.

It gave the guys the opportunity to see some more of the beauty that Jamaica had to offer, that mostly the tourists enjoy and the people who lives in that part of the country. Negril is in the West end of Jamaica and it's very popular with the European and spring break tourists. Many people like Negril because it has the prettiest sunset in the world with all the white sand beaches and beautiful seas. They drove through St, Elizabeth and up Spur Tree and stop in Mandeville where Trinity had a mansion. While driving to Mandeville they stopped and bought melon and shrimp on the way so the guys weren't hungry. Trinity went and picked up some stuff out of his house and he gave the house keeper a wad of cash and then they proceeded to Kingston. They didn't stop in Clarendon but they stopped in Old Harbour Town where they bought fried fish and fried bammy with some natural orange juice.

Passing through Old Harbour and not stopping to buy fish and bammy is the ultimate crime in Jamaican. They drive on until they reached New Kingston about 2pm. The building was situated off Trafalgar Road a few metres from the British High Commission. Spanner said "I don't know how come the British have such beautiful real estates in our country and Jamaican could never have that property in the UK. The British government took Jamaicans for fool and they shouldn't own such beautiful places in Jamaica in the heart of the business district". Trinity replied "I hope to own the British High Commission property one day when a nationalist government chase them out of Jamaica. Just like what Mugabe had done in Zimbabwe and Hugo Chavez did to that Rich British guy who owns some of the best land in Venezuela".

Trinity said, "There is no way the British or Americans should be allowed to own the best properties in a black country". Trinity wasn't too fond of the British or American authorities but he did like their money. At the work site they spent almost five hours before Trinity said he was ready to go by Kitson Town to check on what was happening. Trinity dropped the guys off and then returned to his apartment complex in Norbrook where the former Prime Minister and foreign diplomats lived. Spanner was happy to be back in Kitson Town because he missed his three kids and his kids' mom who was eight months pregnant at the time. Trinity dropped off every one at their gate and told them thanks and then he drove off back toward Kingston. He decided that he would visit his aunt the following day to discuss business.

THE DEATH OF TRINITY

On the Friday night after he let off Spanner and his brother Button, he spent some time with his aunt before he left for Kingston. That evening was the last time anyone from the community would ever see him again. After Trinity stopped at his aunt's gate he got out and left Spanner and Button in the jeep to wait for him. Spanner and Button waited for well over an hour and when they didn't see him coming Spanner decided to walk the 800 metre to his house. Trinity wanted to drop Spanner off at his gate because he was carrying another tower computer when he picked him up in Halfway Tree. Spanner didn't feel any way though, because he knew that Trinity had his business to deal with and he could see Trinity another day. Little did Spanner know that he would never see his friend Trinity again?

The Sunday while Spanner was eating his dinner, which was comprised of rice and peas with chicken and sour-sop juice he heard the news that three men in a grey Nissan Sunny car shot and killed a man in a F150 truck in St Andrew's affluent community, in the area where Trinity had his apartments. He didn't know who it was, so Spanner continued to eat his dinner. Hearing that someone had been murdered was an everyday occurrence but he didn't know that it was his friend, who had been killed. No one knew that it was Trinity who got killed that Sunday evening. Those three guys who killed him had been trailing him for weeks without him knowing it. He didn't give his enemies chances in the States to kill him so how come he was so careless in Jamaica? Only in his coffin, would Spanner be able to see him again for the last time at his funeral.

Jamaica was the last place on earth Trinity expected someone would try to kill him. He did under estimate how cold the killers in Jamaica were. On the Sunday evening three men waited on Trinity near his apartment and then they shot up the truck with him in it, he lost control and the truck crashed into a wall. He ran out of the truck after it crashed and ran toward his apartment calling out for help but there was no one to help him. The security guards at the gate tried to get away from the scene of the shooting but they too were murdered. They followed Trinity to his apartment door where they killed him. No amount of money in the world could help him. They gave him 15 shots all over his body. Before he got killed he was begging for his life to be saved but his plea fell on deaf ears, it was a hit man job and there was no way out for him. He was killed execution style.

They shot him in his forehead and heart to make sure that he was dead. Spanner got the news the Monday morning while he was going to work, that it was Trinity they killed. Spanner and Button were supposed to go and see Trinity on the evening he was killed. It was only because Button's car couldn't start why they didn't bother. It was shocking for Spanner and just about everyone who knew and loved Trinity; it was a very sad day. It was just days ago he was giving away millions of dollars to poor people; unfortunately, none of them was around to help him in his time of need. People were saying that it looked like he knew that he was going to die. The police said that when they arrived on the scene they found (JA$1,000.000) in his truck. The gunmen didn't want his money, they were there to see Trinity dead and that was what they did.

They couldn't kill Trinity in the States so they paid someone to kill him in Jamaica because it was much easier there. The hit was directed from out of New York by one of his business rivals. They didn't rob him of the four or so million that he was carrying around with him when they killed him, because they didn't want his money, they just wanted him dead. They took over some of the drugs business that he left for his friends to run in the US. Trinity's friends retaliated brutally; they killed eighteen men in the States from a rival gang and another fifteen in Jamaica.

Those killed were bankers, accountants, gunmen, drugs dons and other businessmen who got caught up in the web of killing that followed. Five days after Trinity was buried gunmen shot up his brother's house and wounded five family members. It was an all out war after the funeral of Trinity Errol, on an international scale. Another twelve people got murdered in Columbia, eight in the UK, seven in Canada and many more in Jamaica and the States. The killing was so out of control that everyone lost count of the dead and injured.

It was like a killing field out there; it was like the world was coming to an end because the Don Dada was dead. None of his enemies knew who would be next on Trinity's friends' hit list, which was very long. Some of his enemies ran away but they weren't good at hiding and they were hunted down and slaughtered like animals. In Kingston where Trinity used to live, the guys were on lookout and patrolling the street with all types of high powered weaponry. They were ready and waiting on orders to avenge their Dons death, and to kill off the families of all who was involved in Trinity's death. Two policemen strayed into 77 Lane, a community off Waltham Park Road, and they were gunned down like dogs. In Spanish Town and Kitson Town (the other two areas where Trinity once lived) men were on the lookout night and day, well armed with high powered rifles and semi-automatic pistols.

All the areas that Trinity once lived weren't short of arms- because he had seen to it that they were well armed and protected. It was such a pity that he didn't use some of his friends as his body guards. If his friends had the slightest idea that someone wanted to kill him there was no way they would have allowed anyone to get near to him much more to kill him. There was a lot of killing and shooting going on because of his death, and it would be a long time before the killing was over because his friends had vowed revenge. In Jamaica at the General Penitentiary, Spanish Town District Prison and at the Gun Court Remand Centre, gangs were killing each other because of the death of Trinity. There were prisoners who were friends with the people who killed Trinity in all three prisons. That caused war to broke out inside the prisons and Trinity's friends killed off some of his enemies.

It caused riots in the Island prisons and when it was over, 24 prisoners died. Soldiers and police were called in to man the prison and beef up security because the prisoners took over the prisons. Wardens couldn't cope with the killing so they ran out of the prison compound, locking the door behind them. Too much killing and maiming were taking place and many lives were in danger. The wardens treated prisoners badly, and they knew that if the prisoners caught any of them they would be killed. The superintendent (governor) for the General Penitentiary prison was held hostage in the bakery and prisoners were threatening to bake him alive in the oven like bread! The governor was huge but what he was hearing was serious because it was coming from some of Jamaica's most fearsome career criminals. The governor sweated profusely and pissed his pants. He begged for his life, like children begged for candies.

Five wardens were killed in the riot; the governor at the time didn't read the riot act because if he did the soldiers and police could start shooting prisoners and he didn't want that to happen. Anyway, things were getting out of hand, so the soldiers had to kill one of the prisoners who they said attacked them, to show that they were now in charge of the prison and they were serious. The security force calmed things down on the second day of the riot, but the situation was still tense. During the situation in the prison there were negotiations going on for the releasing of the number two governor, (he was called 'Make-sure') while in other parts of the prison, prisoners were still looting and trying to cause as much destruction as possible. The situations in Jamaica prison are deplorable and the prisoners got an excuse to vent their grievance during the riot.

The riot happened because Trinity was dead. All the food, clothes, tools and equipment that was in the store was looted and most of the loot thrown over GP's ten foot wall. All the stuff in the prison store was sold on the outside, and the funniest thing was that the soldiers helped the prisoners to smuggle the goods out! Soldiers were manning the sentry boxes, so they were able to direct goods over the wall to be sold on the outside whilst a geezer called 'Trafficater' was busy trafficking weed over the prison wall!

Spanner said: "When no weed is inside Jamaica's prisons, the prisoner's war against each other and sometimes attack wardens. In foreign prisons, it's the heroin and the cocaine that keeps them calm. The government and warden know that without drugs in prison, it would be mayhem". There were four ghettos around GP prison, the deadliest prison in Jamaica, and the prisoners used them to their advantage by throwing light stuff over the wall for their friends and family to sell. Things were getting from bad to worse, so the authority had to draw a line and bring back law and order in the prison.

A few days later, calm were back in the prisons and the riots were over. Trinity was the cause of the GP prison riot, but many of the prisoners used the opportunity to put across all their grievances and frustrations to the minister of justice. 'Chinaman' was there during the riot and he said: "the authority was feeding them with yam" for breakfast, dinner and tea everyday for over five months". Chinaman was one of Trinity's best friends, they had spent time in prison together and Chinaman was now waiting on his parole. With the murder of their friend Trinity; and the inhuman treatment that they were getting caused the rude boys to get mad. It was like a time bomb waiting to be exploded and when Trinity died it just erupted like a bloody volcano. When the riots were over, it left death and destruction behind and millions of dollars worth of damage.

Some of the rioters ended up getting life sentences for the murders they committed during the rampage inside the prisons.

There were murders in America prisons in the States because Trinity's enemies were all over the place and it was payback time. It didn't stop there, because bodies were being shipped down to Jamaica from America and Canada. They found two bodies in Holland at the Rotterdam Port in suitcases destined for Jamaica. Trinity was big with the Dutch Mafia who was led by a dread from Jamaica called Butter- because he was very slippery. While in the UK, the cops found headless bodies over the docklands which was the signature of the Yardman. The

Yardman was an affiliate of the Shower Posse. Trinity was friend with Blake who was the head of the Shower Posse.

Trinity and Spanner had lots of friends who were members of the Shower Posse and the Yardy gangs. In Canada, eight bodies were found in a container that was bound for Jamaica. There were also four bodies at Kingston wharf in barrels. At other prisons in the States 17 prisoners were killed. All those killings were over the death of Trinity the Don of all Dons in Jamaica. He paid the price by getting himself killed but he left death and destruction behind. In a community called 'Moscow' in Trench Town, his friends killed every dog they saw because they didn't catch one of the main masterminds behind Trinity's murder.

Lots of people got caught up in the violence that followed Trinity's death, even long after his burial the killing continued. There were FBI agents who came to Jamaica to investigate what was going on, and to investigate who was linked with all the killing in the USA and Jamaica. Sadly two FBI agents stray in Spanish Town and were gunned down for spying. They and the Jamaican cops' were working together by going to all the night clubs in Kingston that Spanner and Trinity used to frequent.

Can you imagine the Jamaican police being so honest and not stealing some of the dead man's money that they said they found? It was one of Jamaica's most corrupted cops that found the cash, everyone knew that God would have to come first for him to hand over all the cash that he found. Trinity's brother Button said "my brother withdrawn (JA$5,000.000) on the Friday and he drove around with the money in his truck".

Some of the family stopped talking to each other because of Trinity's money. All the equipment on his farm in Portland was stolen because everyone was fighting and didn't have the time to secure them. During the family fighting, Trinity's grave site was being prepared by his loyal friends who saw to it that he was buried beside his grandmother as he requested before he got killed; he had also told his friends that whenever time he died he wanted to be buried besides his granny in the same yard that he grew up in as a child.

There were truck loads of drinks and liquor supplied everyday for the people who were working and mourning the death of Trinity. Loads of food was prepared everyday to feed the hundreds of people who attended the grave side daily. While some women, men and children were working some were also telling jokes and stories about Trinity and his grandmother. His grave was like a luxurious mansion. Trinity's grave was one of the best Spanner had ever seen- and he had attended many Dons and rich people funerals. His grave was tiled inside and out with burglar bars around it and electric lights inside it. Trinity's grave was designed beautifully so that people from all over the world could visit and see where he was buried. The grave has its own electric meter to show how much power it used.

The landscaping work was superb; they planted coconut plants along with flowers to make the place look beautiful. That was his wish and he got it. He was buried in a sepulchre which was a sight to behold. Lots of people from all over the world attended his funeral and there were lots of limos, which took other Dons to bid Trinity farewell. The wake was massive with people from all over the island, the US and UK. There were thousands of people at the wake with food and liquor in abundance. Dons from all over came, some to pay their last respect, while some attended to celebrate silently. Spanner did expect to see more people at the wake though, because of the amount of cash Trinity gave away days before he was killed.

Spanner said "that is to show people that money can't buy happiness or make people like you." At the wake Trinity's family killed five cows, twelve goats, eight pigs and two tons of chicken. It was the sending off party of the century with truck loads of drinks and liquor for everyone to mourn or celebrate. Lots of people were afraid to attend the wake and funeral for safety reasons. Some were saying that the men who killed Trinity would come back to shoot up the wake and funeral and kill more people. Those sorts of thing happened in Jamaica all the time, so people were aware and constantly on the lookout. The wake took place without any incident likewise the funeral, a day later. The wake took place on Saturday night and the funeral took place on Sunday evening.

While the funeral was taking place there were some strange cars driving through the area that the people didn't recognise and that made the citizens uncomfortable and fearful for their lives. They were saying that the guys in the strange cars were gunmen who had come to shoot up the funeral and kill the rest of Trinity's family but that never happened. The service took place and lots of people from all over the world came to bid Trinity farewell. The Dons were out in droves, in their limos, and drinking the finest champagne, while dressed in their expensive designer suits.

The funeral was like a fashion show, with ladies wearing the latest designs and with their best hair styles on display. After the funeral was over, there were parties all over the place where people could go and enjoy themselves. The main dance was held at the Barry & Lloyd Community Centre that was run by Spanner.

The planning of Trinity Death

He did get the chance to fulfil his dreams of being filthy rich and famous, unfortunately, he died a young man. He was only 42 years old when he got murdered and he spent almost 20 years out of his life in prison. Trinity never smoke or drank and he had little time for fun but when he got in the mood he surely knew how to party. He liked to ride his CBR motor bike and he was very skilful at it, and he also enjoyed fast cars of which he had many. But most of all enjoyed making money because that was his main hobby. The ladies loved him, but he wasn't the type of guy who a woman could pin down and look to for marriage. Trinity trusted the ladies more than his men friend; after all, the ladies could only steal some cash from him which was nothing to him, but he knew that they would be always there for him in time of need also. The men, on the other hand, were good for security purposes, but they sometimes got greedy like Judas. And we all knew what Judas did to Christ.

The men may not have been that reliable, but he could depend on them when things get tough, and that's exactly what happened after he was murdered. Trinity was very busy dealing with his many businesses, and at one stage he didn't have any time for his girlfriend Tanya. That caused her to get upset, and when things got out of hand she set up his life with her former lover. Trinity planned to marry Tanya after he finished with the drug business. Trinity didn't keep his part of the deal and that played a part in the breaking down of their relationship. Tanya returned to the States where she set up Trinity life. She was madly in love with Trinity and couldn't afford to lose him to another woman so she helped to get him killed. Three months later after Trinity was killed, his friend drove by one of the hit-man business place, and gunned him down with two of his cronies.

Jacqular was one of the men in the hit man car on that Sunday evening when Trinity was murdered. He was hired by Wally. Jacqular used to be Tanya's boyfriend and she also knew Wally who lived in the same area in New York. She made the connection with the two to kill Trinity. Jacqular was an area don for the PNP, he was ruthless, he also owned and ran his own business and he controlled lots of gunmen. Two days after he killed Trinity, he bought a brand new BMW X5 Jeep. Jacqular didn't get enough time to enjoy his BMW or the money that he got because he was gunned down on his corner in front of his business before his friends and family. Jacqular was a geezer who couldn't be trusted, because he ripped off the Colombians and was in hiding. He couldn't return to any foreign countries, even the Russians got ripped off by him in New York and everyone wanted him dead.

He was happy to take the hit man job but little did he know that he was playing with fire. It was the wrong man he chose to kill so he had to pay back with his own life. Jacqular was a well respected don in Kingston where he ran the ghetto in the heart of the city. When Jacqular got killed, his funeral was one of the biggest. All the dons from Jamaica and foreign attended and sent him off in style. His coffin was filled with money, gold and champagne. Jacqular's funeral was the fashion show of the century. He messed with a richer don than him, Jacqular's death was similar to Trinity's but the only difference was that Trinity was more powerful internationally and was wealthier but they all died by the gun. Jacqular's funeral was bigger than Trinity's because he was a regular on the party scene, and every club owner and entertainers knew him.

Jacqular's funeral was the talk of the town for months. It wasn't long after Jacqular was buried, Trinity's friends caught up with the other two guys who were in the car with Jacqular on the Sunday evening that they gunned down Trinity. They were taken out of their beds away from their girlfriends and shot in the back of the head on Spanish Town Road. They were left to rot in May Pen Cemetery in the pauper section. The men throats were cut and their tongues pulled through the cut on the neck to make it look like a neck tie. In the underworld it's known as a Colombian neck tie. No mercy was shown to those who killed Trinity or who were involved in his death.

The three contract killers were now dead. They were from the Kingston 12 area, one of the most dangerous places to live in Jamaica.

The last two killers were found with their hands tied behind them, they were also blind folded and stray dogs and pigs were eating their rotting bodies. They died like dogs and no one mourned their death. They were terrorists in the area that they lived and Jacqular employed them to do all his dirty work. They were treated like nobody in the Jungle area of Arnett Garden Kingston 12. When people heard of their death they all rejoiced and all the women were celebrating that the two rapists were dead. A young man commented "now all the women are free to go about their business without anything happening to them".

There was this big gathering to discuss their death when a woman shouted: "mi glad say dem dead because every woman can now sleep without their knickers." The crowd broke into laughter. One woman said "it's true because I used to be afraid to sleep without mi draws on," "It was like a party to see how the people were happy". "I am glad someone got rid of those two thugs that were like a curse on the community" said a fat lady. May Pen Cemetery is on the border line between Tivoli Garden JLP and Greenwich PNP Farm communities. On the other side of Spanish Town you have Arnett Garden a People National Party strong hold and where the three hoodlums came from. Some youths were walking through the cemetery when they saw some dogs fighting and they went to investigate what was going on, and they found the two bodies.

They called the police who called Madden funeral parlour who had a contract with the government to bury the dead. They were buried in the paupers section of the cemetery without a funeral service. No post mortem was performed because they were so badly decomposed. Rumour had it that everyone, especially the women in and around West Kingston, Kingston 10 and 12 area, were celebrating for weeks without wearing knickers.

Three weeks later Tanya was found in her apartment in New York, hanging, a suicide note with all the names of the people who were involved in Trinity's death and why she did it, was found on a table. She took her life, so it seemed, but Trinity's friends knew better than that. The letter said "I loved Trinity too much to lose him" and how she couldn't live without him". Tanya continued in the letter "I took my own life so that I could be with Trinity in paradise". She said "Trinity was going to leave me after all they had been through and I couldn't face it".

She continued "it was too much for me to bear so I had to contact Wally and make a deal with him to kill Trinity. I contacted my ex-lover Jacqular and made arrangements on how to get Trinity killed" She said " I was very sorry and at least none of them will be around to go through the agony of breaking up" Tanya was the last one to die in the first wave of death after Trinity got killed. It would be another seven years before the spiral of death ended. Suzie was out of sight and out of mind, but what was she thinking or doing? Everything seemed to be back to normal and all the family that got caught up in the violence was carrying on with their lives. Some continued fighting for the things Trinity died and left. The last three years were like living in Gaza.

Trinity the story teller

The death of Trinity caused much grief and pain which left many family and friends in mourning. Here are some stories Trinity would share with his friends. While in the General Penitentiary there was this warden (screw) by the name of John McFarlane. John McFarlane was the same warden who hit Spanner in his head with a baton after he and another prisoner had a fight. He was a wicked warden and prisoners didn't like him so they set up a plan that would change the way he treated them for good. This screw was a problem to all inmates and enjoyed terrorising them.

He loved his belly and was very greedy and loved to eat out prisoner's food when they cooked their pot. One day, some prisoners killed a John Crow, a scavenger bird that eats dead meat and cooked it like chicken and gave it to John McFarlane to eat. He ate it and enjoyed it too; he even commented that it was the nicest chicken meat he had ever eaten. The prisoners were having a laugh at the screw's expense. News got around the prison that he ate the scavenger bird and he was embarrassed. Hence, he got the name John-Crow-McFarlane. From that day onward that warden was never a problem to the prisoners again. He just went about his business holding down his head in shame.

There was this other warden by the name of Marsh but prisoners called him 'food tray'. The reason for that was because he would always guard prisoner's food like hawk. There was this one time when a prisoner took an extra plate of food and he was beaten to death for it. This warden 'Food Tray' was wicked to the extreme, and he always told prisoners that if it was in his power he would feed the prison population with one grain of rice. Trinity used to be a very good story teller and his stories would sometimes deter others from going into crime and prison.

Then there was this other warden who was always drunk and beating up prisoners, he was a sergeant. He was the one guarding Jim Brown the night when he died in a fire on F-Wing.

He was so drunk that he didn't even hear the alarm. Or maybe he heard it and didn't care. He was never charged for his crime of sleeping on the job, a warden could kill prisoners and not get into any trouble, and prisoners were received in GP as a body. Maybe someone should call for a national inquiry into all the deaths that happened in GP prison during the 1980s. How many wardens would be charged for murder, many? All the murders that took place during 1982-1990 didn't get investigated by the authorities that supervise Jamaican prisons. Jamaican prisons during the 1980s were one of the worst in the world. Death was a weekly occurrence in GP on Tower Street in Kingston.

Trinity was now dead but his name still lives on and some of his dreams still continue. Because of his death lots of people think that they got away with the money he lent them but they were in for a surprise. He died and left millions for his not so loving family and friends to fight over. The murder and shooting were over for the time being and a new wind was blowing in the air until Suzie decided that it was time to make her final bid for all Trinity's assets.

There were lots of youths from the areas Trinity used to live and frequent, some vowed to follow in his footsteps while other were up for revenge. Trinity was a role model and a motivator to many and although he was now dead he had left his influence on many people.

On the Monday morning after the news that Trinity had been killed, the people from Kitson Town blocked the road in protest of his killing. In Sea view Garden in Kingston 11, three police cars was burned out, and there were shoot outs with the police, soldiers and gunmen for most of the day. Spanish Town Road and Waltham Park Road were all blocked while the police and gunmen fought running gun battles. In the end six gunmen and two police were killed, with score of other being injury.

The second wave of killing continued

One week after Spanner was freed and back in Jamaica, they killed one of Trinity brother Button, the one who was in the jeep on the evening Trinity picked up Spanner on Half Way Tree Road. The District of Old Road was shocked again, for the second time in seven years, with the killing of Trinity's brother Button. That brother used to help with Trinity's affairs at one stage or another.

In 2005, three men were murdered at Nail shop down by Old Road Bottom by gunmen, who were trying to get rid of all Trinity's friends and associate, the guys were at the shop playing dominoes when the shooting took place. The killing frenzy was gradually creeping back into the community, which was a concern to the citizens. During the killing spree one of Spanner friend, Reagan was gunned down in Patsy's shop in Kitson Town. Spanner once used to run his Golden Jerk and restaurant at My Father's Place, the same premises Reagan was murdered. Some people were saying that if Spanner was around things like that wouldn't or couldn't happen. Spanner was an enforcer in his community and he wielded his influence all over Jamaica because he was a political activist and he was known all over the island. Spanner was no push over and don't forget that he learnt his skills on the street of Kingston.

In the same year, another five men were murdered in Kitson Town by gunmen, who drove through randomly shooting up the area. There were also seven murders in 2003/2004 that were all linked to Trinity's death. Not to be out done by these people, Trinity's friends retaliated thus, there was further bloodshed across Jamaica again for the second time after his death. News reaching Spanner that Devil was also gunned down by a rival gang. It seems like the killing wasn't going to stop. Something would have to be done and fast.

In Kingston 12, where Trinity's killers came from, two car loads with men armed with high powered automatic rifles went to one of the killer's home and killed his children and their mother. On their way out of Kingston, the police and military patrol tried to stop them but they shoot their way out, leaving two policemen and a soldier dead. It didn't stop there, because they also went to Spanish Town and killed four more men on the train line who were involved in the Kitson Town murders. They burned down four houses and two cars that were alleged to be involved in the drive by shooting in Old Road and Kitson Town.

Spanner the fixer

Spanner visited the murder scene to see what took place and he saw that Button was shot between his eyes, just like what had been done to Jacqular in his coffin. There was also a shot in his mouth too as if to stop him from talking. He was killed execution style, like his brother Trinity. Spanner wasn't really worried about his safety, because he knew that for anyone to get to him they would have to ambush him, and that was hard to do. He grew up in Kitson Town where everyone knew him and most of the people were his relatives, even the kids knew him well because he always organised Christmas parties for them. Any suspicious movement in the community would be reported to him and he would know what to do next.

Spanner knew Kitson Town like the back of his hands and he didn't leave his head back that careless. He tried to avoid getting drawn into the revenge thing, but things were getting from bad to worse and he had to put a stoppage to it. The Jamaica Labour Party MP and PNP caretaker requested Spanner's help which he accepted gracefully. It was a fact that when Spanner was around, there was no crime and before he went to the UK there was no crime or murder in Kitson Town. Spanner would have to prove his leadership and authority for everyone to see, that would be when he took things into his hands. The politicians didn't know what to do, but Spanner assured them that he would see to it that things cooled down. Politicians were the first people to handout guns to political activist during 1970; they started the problem, and were not able to stop it.

Trinity's murder didn't make it any easier for Spanner to stop the killing that was going on. He grew up in the city and knew all the in and out of ghetto running, so he was the right person who could help bring peace and stop the killing. The first thing Spanner did was to call a meeting with his friends in the city and some of his area men in Kitson Town. After the meeting was finished, it was time for action. Spanner knew how to get the killing to stop but first he would have to set an example. Killing Trinity's brother Button was disrespectful, and someone would have to pay, big time. The cops came to ask Spanner to help them stop the killing, but he told them that he couldn't promise them anything. Suzie was Trinity's ex-girlfriend and she was the one fuelling the wave of killing out of greed.

Spanner said "if Suzie gets killed all the killing would have to stop because there was no one else with a grudge". The day before Trinity's brother got killed he was with Suzie and she accused him of holding onto Trinity's properties and money. Suzie wasn't short of money because she had already robbed Trinity of forty million Jamaican dollars from his rental car business and thousands of acres of land, yet she still wanted more. Button told her to go to hell because she robbed Trinity so she ordered him killed. Spanner knew that Button and Suzie never saw eye to eye all though the years while they were fighting to control Trinity's businesses when he was in prison.

Button used to run his brother's businesses while he was in prison, but something went down and Trinity turned over the business to Suzie. She and her son took over from Button and that was when she saw the opportunity to steal Trinity's money. Button and the rest of family didn't like Suzie so it caused lots of bad blood. She wasn't satisfied with what she and her son stole, so she got Button killed. People in the community of Kitson Town knew what had happened the day before he got killed, so it was obvious who did it. Spanner knew all that was going on because he was well informed of pass and present activities, before he left Jamaica and when he returned. He knew the only way to stop the killing was to get Suzie and her family killed, so he ordered a hit on the whole family. Spanner stated "as of next week I don't want to see anymore killing over Trinity's properties".

He gave out the order to kill Suzie and her family and to burn out their houses and businesses. Suzie's son Shutz was the first one to get killed, while on Waltham Park Road in Kingston. He was Suzie's only child and she loved him with all her heart, so the strategy was to kill him and everyone she loved. Shutz, had stopped at a stop light at Molynes Road and Waltham Park Road intersection and he was shot in the head. While waiting on the light to change, a bike rode up to his sport car, knocked on the window and then shot him through his ear, he died on the spot. Jucky Jam return to base with the news that Shutz was killed. Spanner and some of his boys were drinking Dragon Stout when Jucky Jam came into the room and said "boss the job is accomplished". Spanner clapped his hands and said "so far one down, let the war begin".

Rat posing as a delivery man knocked on Suzie's door, and when she opened the door, she was shot between her eyes. Later that same evening two group of guys went to Suzie's father's place of business and they murdered him and set fire to his supermarket. It didn't stop there because; Suzie's house in Cherry gardens was burned to the ground. Her shopping centre, petrol station and her mother's house were all burned down. Suzie's mother was burned up in her house. In all there were 24 people who got murdered that Saturday night.

There were millions worth of damage to properties. Suzie wanted all Trinity's money; she couldn't be satisfied with what she had stolen, so she lost all, including her life and beloved family. It was stated in the news that it was the worst weekend of violence in Jamaica since they started recording such incidents. The news reached Spanner that all was accomplished and he was pleased. On the Sunday morning the news reached Kitson Town that Trinity's ex-girlfriend and her whole family were murdered. It was joy for some who love and worshipped Trinity's but for some they felt it was not worth the loss of so many lives. There were talking all over about what might have happened and who could have done it, but no one called Spanner's name. Days, weeks and months passed without anymore killing.

Suzie was dead and she died as a result of the violence she perpetrated. A week later Button was buried in the family plot with his brother and grandmother. After Suzie's death, everyone found out that she was behind Button's death and the rest of killing that was going on. She wanted her hands on all of Trinity's wealth but she died without enjoying what she had stolen. As for his so-called friend who stole his bike, car and money, his head was found in Westmoreland and his body in Portland. His business was burnt out. What Spanner wanted, was peace and happiness for everyone in his community and he got it in the end.

The cop who found the money in Trinity's truck was the cop who asked him if he wanted protection. This cop has a bad reputation and couldn't be trusted. He was mixed up in drugs, extortion and killing so-called bad men innocently. This cop even killed his own nephew because he was a gunman. To add insult to injury he took his nephew dead body in the police car to his sister home and ask her to look what he have in the trunk of his car.

His sister was surprised to see her own son in the trunk of her brother police car, dead with multiple gunshot wounds. She fainted. Magul as he was called was an executioner in the Jamaican police force. He was so corrupt that a former police commissioner had to move him from front line duty and gave him a desk job because of his disgraceful behaviour in the force. During the commissioners reign he took all the criminal cops in the Jamaican police force off the street and gave them a desk job and fired some and asked others to resign.

It was after the People National Party came back into power they fired the commissioner and the rouge cops were given back their reign to murder, continue with extortion and all manner of evil again. Some of those police including Magul became senior (Superintendent) criminals in the police force and still are today. So here Jamaica has the blind leading the blind because most of those cops aren't intelligent enough. They got their jobs some 30 years ago when policing wasn't so sophisticated and it didn't required intelligence to join the police force. One of those famous cops' now retired after over a dozen questionable murders and he have the gall to want to be commissioner of police.

Did Magul know something about Trinity death, if not why would he tell Trinity that people wanted to killed him, or was he in on the killing? He was the first cops on the scene after the killing. Trinity's brother after he got the news went straight to his brother's apartment and took out all the cash that was hidden in the house. Before Trinity came from the States to Jamaica he sent down (US$50,000.000) fifty million in cash with some girls, in paintings and other disguises that he employed to evade customs. Some of the cash was transported in many different ways with different people. No one knows where some of that cash went but what they did know was that some of his family hit the jackpot, big time.

Trinity's money was just floating all around the place, there were so many people who had money for him, but he was now dead. Most of the money he had in the bank went to the government because he didn't put it in someone else's name or make a 'Will'. Lots of people got rich out of Trinity, some didn't even like him when he was growing up but they surely liked his money. It wasn't long before his possessions were shared up amongst family who weren't there for him when he was down and out, but they were the ones who got some of his millions. It took Button days to clear out the furniture from his apartment. There were lots of infighting going on over Trinity stuff which including some of the finest Italian furniture and clothes some of them had ever seen.

Some mourners went to church while some went to the pub and the others went to party. On the day of the funeral, it was the saddest day in the history of the community because the one person, who was going to uplift the community once more, was dead.

Trinity did left Jamaica a poor young man and he returned a very rich and powerful man, but he was now dead. The children and old people cried because he loved and cared for the young and old. Trinity wasn't even cold in his grave, before people started to fight for his possessions. There were threats all over the place that if they didn't get what they wanted, what and what they would do. Family and so-called friends were holding onto what they already had with no intention of handing them over. It was a disgrace to see what was going on because it wasn't even a month since Trinity died and the family was already at war. His burial place was the prettiest in the community and lots of people went to look at it and take pictures. It was a monument in the area for everyone to see. It wasn't nice to see what was going on with Trinity's things but such is life. Spanner marvelled over the situation but refused to get involved in the family dispute.

A monument was all that was left of Trinity for everyone who knew him to see and marvel at. Anyone who drove, walked or rode on the Corner Lane Road could see the grave where Trinity was (buried in the same yard where he grew up as a young boy). He once lived and played in the yard he was buried in, and that's the sad fact everyone who knew him would have to live with. Surprisingly, many of the people who he helped didn't even remember him or the good he had done. Spanner said, "I bet some will be quick to say that he lived by the gun and he died by it". Trinity was gunned down executioner style on his apartment complex at his flat door, and everyone knew that it was a hit job.

Guanaboa Vale and modern day slavery

After Guanaboa Vale lost its status as the town for all the communities around it, Old Road were the district that reigned supreme. It was after the death of the shop owner that the district went into decline. Some would argue that Trinity was the one who robbed the shop and because of him, the owner died of a heart attack in hospital. While others would argue, that Trinity was the one who was developing Old Road to take back its rightful place as the dominant community in and around Guanaboa Vale. Apart from Trinity, Spanner was the only other person who wanted to do something good for his community.

It was no surprise when Trinity returned to Jamaica a rotten rich man. The guy was spending money like he was the Bank of Jamaica. A property owner Mr Adrian Walsh was in the same age group as Trinity, but Trinity make him look stupid where money was concerned. Adrian Walsh inherited the property that so many slaves got murdered on during the days of slavery, from his dad who got it from his dad also. All the owners were and still are slave masters using natives for cheap labour. Trinity was so proud to return back to his community to liberate his people. Lots of people from the surrounding communities stopped working with the property owner and started working for Trinity on his many construction sites. It was modern day slavery on the white man's property, but Trinity paid a better wage.

The property owner had thousands of acres of land, but he didn't have the millions of US dollars in raw cash that Trinity had. To get that kind of money Adrian Walsh would have to sell off some of his land or borrow some money from Trinity, Trinity was just waiting to step in and take it off his hands but Mr Walsh wasn't interested in selling any of his property at the time. This white guy would sometimes drive into the community of Old Road, just to look at the scale of construction that was going on and size up his opposition. He was losing workers to this guy who had just come from nowhere to give him a run for his money. Adrian Walsh property surrounded all the communities around his property so he thought that he had the right to do as he pleased but he got a nasty surprise with the arrival of Trinity.

In Guanaboa Vale all the talk was about Trinity and to a lesser extent Spanner, who Adrian Walsh feared, even the Guanaboa Vale police feared him.

Spanner and Trinity didn't like to know that their community people were being robbed of their property, so they were not particularly pleased with Adrian Walsh. Adrian Walsh didn't like them either because he knew that they were a threat to him, nevertheless, he had to live with them anyway. Walsh was classed as a law abiding citizen, but Trinity and Spanner had been outlaws. An outlaw can do as they please and don't particularly care, what happens after is anyone guess, that's the reality of a don. Taking on the state isn't a problem for a don, when it happens it sometimes leaves many poor people dead, or murdered by the state like in Tivoli Garden.

Some of Trinity and Spanner's relatives and school mates worked with the Walsh's (both mother and son), so it would be hard for a conspiracy to plot against the two guys, who weren't any fools. Trinity wasn't bothered about Adrian Walsh, but he did want to buy out some of his property because he had the best land around, some of it was idling and doing nothing. Trinity said: "if I could get a few hundred acres of Walsh land to develop, Kitson Town and Old Road, then I would build the model community I always dreamt about as a boy. One white boy had all the land around the community that they lived on and because of that, Guanaboa Vale, Kitson Town and Old Road can't be developed."

Lots of people were upset with Adrian Walsh for this reason. One of Spanner's school friends Rusty had to give this boy, Adrian Walsh, a proper beating one evening by his petrol station after school. He always thought because he was rich he could do as he liked and get away with it.

Rusty was now in the USA doing 75 years for killing four DEA and two CIA agents. The hit on the agents was sanctioned by Trinity, Rusty was his number one hit man and he went all over the US killing Trinity's enemies. As a hit man he was very professional and he never disobeyed Trinity's orders. There was this particular time while he was in Miami supervising the distribution of a ton of cocaine. He was placed in front of the building with the drugs, on the top floor with his sniper rifle pointing at the front door of the house with the coke.

There came the DEA swooping down on the house. He fired four shots and when it was over, three of the agents were lying dead on the ground and the fourth one was paralyzed from the neck down. The fourth agent was shot in his neck. All three agents got shot through the head. Rusty wasn't a fan of authority (cops) and his theory was 'killing pussy, he killed them for fun." From school days Rusty wasn't someone to play with. He was Spanner's friend and Spanner was the one who introduced him to Trinity. Rusty went to the US on a farm work program and he ran away from his contract and headed to New York where some of Spanner's friends were living. He contacted Spanner and he was linked up with Trinity.

After that evening, Adrian made sure he avoided getting into fights around his property because he knew the local youths would always get the better of him. He did apply for a gun license which he got in record time because he was rich and white. Maybe he had an automatic right to a gun because of the privilege of his upbringing and white background. For God's sake this guy was the descendant of a slave master so it wouldn't be surprising if he carried a gun without a license! The police station, Post Office, was on Adrian Walsh property along with the petrol station, so he had the police at Guanaboa Vale station eating out of his hands, and he knew that he could get away with a lot of things. The Guanaboa Vale All Age School was on Anglican Church land which was given by the property owners during the days of slavery, he leased most of the remaining church property because his family made big donations to the church.

That's the kind of influence this geezer had over the rule of law in and around the communities that his property surrounded. The thing about Jamaica was that even though people knew Adrian Walsh background, they all accepted that he was a Jamaican. Calling Adrian a 'white boy' wasn't racist, everyone accepted him as one of 'us' because he grew up with all the black kids, but he was a spoilt brat and Jamaicans hated that. It should be noted that Jamaicans were not really bothered about skin colour. As a nation everyone is supposed to be equal in theory but in practice corruption sometimes caused unfairness. Jamaica's motto is: **Out of many one people.**

No one would say 'white boy go back from where your fore parents came'. Maybe they were from Scotland, Wales or even England but that didn't matter. Black Jamaicans accepted the fact that he was a true Jamaican. Walsh's mother was a nurse in the UK before she came to Jamaica and she worked for free helping the sick people in and around Guanaboa Vale. 'Nursey' as she was called, was a good white woman, everyone loved and respected her. Spanish Town hospital was over eight miles away, so whenever someone got a cut or felt unwell, Mrs Walsh was the first and nearest person they would turn to for help.

This factor helped Adrian Walsh because his dad and mom were not bad employers, although Adrian was. Spanner and Trinity once went to get help as youngster from Mrs Walsh after getting cuts and bruises while playing. Because they always remembered the kindness of his mom they were never interested in picking a fight with Adrian. People were telling him that Spanner wanted to take away his gun, but he never showed Spanner any bad face. On the contrary, he saw Spanner many times near his property, and he always said hello and never tried to disrespect him.

Spanner Living it up in New Kingston

It should be noted that Spanner and Mice were sparring buddies during the three years he spend living in upper St Andrew aka uptown Kingston. Spanner and Mice went to the Asylum night club, every night, apart from Monday when the club was closed. Mice was the one who introduced Spanner to The Killer, Mr Welsh, Champagne, Christ, Rat, Dog and many more big hitters on the uptown party scene. Trinity was not the type of guy to show off or big up himself, but all these other guys loved the lime light. Trinity was the coolest one and by far the richest. Most of these guys had three or more of the latest cars and were known all over Kingston party scene as the men with the most money to spend in all the night clubs. 'Champagney' would put JA$50,000 behind the counter every night at Asylum Night club for the champagne; Spanner and the crew would drink.

Spanner and his friends ruled the party circuit uptown and they would get all the beautiful girls and they were allowed in all the night clubs free. Every night they slept with a different woman and these guys always wore the latest designer gear. In front of the Asylum night club on both sides of Knutsford Boulevard, their cars would be parked. Guys would line up to watch the cars and wash them for JA$100 each which was nothing for the owners to pay them. Mice and his friends didn't pay to go into any of the clubs or major dancehall because the guys spent thousands of dollars on drinks when they got inside, so whenever they showed up at a dance, party or clubs they were let in without any question. On the night of the Jamaica Reggae Boyz qualified in 1998 for France football world cup tournament, Spanner, Mice, Killer and the rest of the guys drove around and celebrated Jamaica's success. They sprayed each other with Champagne.

At these dances, sessions, parties and clubs, the FBI would be there secretly gathering information. The DEA, FBI and Jamaican Detectives were video recording the movement of the Dons and all the others players. These Dons were spending money like there was no tomorrow. They used champagne to wash their cars and used it to spray on their friends when celebrating birthdays or happy occasions. The dons also burned £50 notes when showing how rich they are. The agents noted all the activities and it would sometimes come back to haunt the Dons when they got caught in the States and they went on trial. These video records would be shown to the judges and it would result in some of the guys getting long sentences. Talking about extradition, Spanner said: "I can't understand why Jamaica gave up its citizens so easily to America and England. America can just send a piece of paper saying 'A and B signed statement on C and Jamaica just hand over 'C' without putting up a fight". That's what Spanner call selling out the country.

The CIA, DEA and FBI would always use the evidence that they gathered whenever the Dons got caught for any crime in the States. Some dons even picked up 112 years without any parole. That's what happened to Curry Puss after killing two DEA officers. Jamaicans didn't play with the Feds, but when the Feds caught any of them the courts always sent them to prison for a very long time. It's a must for Jamaicans to get big sentence in the US or UK, whether they were guilty or not. Sometimes Interpol, the FBI, and the CIA worked with the Jamaican police to catch some of these men. The Jamaican government would praise the cops and their foreign counterparts on their efforts, which annoyed the gangsters and dons.

There were also police who were leaking information to Trinity's friends. Even lawyers were making a killing from extradition cases. The FBI, Interpol and CIA were dealing with a major Jamaican international link that involved drugs, guns, money laundering and murder. The crimes they were investigating had never been seen before because no other crime syndicates had ever killed babies, whilst wiping out a family in drugs war. Jamaicans don't leave any stone un-turn when they go to kill someone, if a child is around, that child would be killed also. Look what happened in Kingston when Trinity's friend locked everyone in the house and burned it down to the ground while blocking the road and engaging the police in a shootout? They didn't care and the American and Interpol knew who they were dealing with so they took special precautions. By letting Jamaican police deal with the matter while they were able to stay in the background.

It wouldn't be anything to kill the Agents, but they would have to get a tip off from the Airport first. Because of what happened, things were put in place to get information from the airport to know when police, CIA, DEA and Interpol were coming to Jamaica to investigate a case, so that they could kill them as they drove out of the airport. Jamaica's dons could not be taken for fools because if the opportunities arose they would kill foreign cops without hesitating. Trinity and the rest of guys called American and British cop's pig's and would kill them if they knew where they were staying or when they come to Jamaica . What the cops were encountering was only seen in some gangster movies but never been played out in real life situation until the Jamaican came on the scene. It wasn't long before some of the international cops started getting murdered in real life situations. In gangster movies the cops didn't get killed but in Jamaica they did every month! Killing police was stale news in Jamaica because sometime two or three would get killed for a month but on average 14 cops got killed each year.

The Don's had a meeting in Kitson Town and they put up a £20, 000 ransom for killing DEA, CIA, and FBI agents, Interpol and Jamaican cops. They were saying that some of the agencies had a hand in setting up Trinity's life and helped to stir up the war that was going on. It was just like what the CIA had done in Columbia before they killed Pablo Escobar. With some of the Dons worrying about their safety, some were returning back to the States and the UK to hide. Some were caught at the airports and were put in prison for crimes committed before Trinity's death. As the saying goes 'you run out of the frying pan and ran straight into the fire' because some ended up doing big bird in federal prisons.

Tit for tat

At one stage of the investigation, agents from the US came to Jamaica and kidnapped one of Trinity's friends and took him back to the States for trial on drugs trafficking and money laundering charge. They couldn't wait on the Jamaican government to extradite him, so he was kidnapped and taken to America where he was tried and received 38 years without parole. The kidnapping caused the Jamaican government to protest to the US government.

It wasn't long after that, that the dons in Jamaica kidnapped an American female journalist; no one has ever heard anything about her since despite, an international man hunt for her. The CIA and Interpol were out in Jamaica in large numbers with all kinds of specialists and dogs searching for the American without any success. Seems she just vanished into thin air!

Her father and mother were in Jamaica appealing for help; it was a revenge for kidnapping the Jamaicans and taking them to the US to face prison. The person who was responsible for setting up Trinity's death; had his family wiped out, all eleven of them were killed, butcher style "like lambs to the slaughter." There were two babies and their grandparents in the house, but Trinity friends still killed and burned down the house, regardless. The father, mother, two brothers, three sisters, grand ma, grand pa and two babies were all in the house when the gang visited. Imagine the sight of the burned bodies around the burnt out building? It was like a bomb had gone off. The smell of roasted skin hung heavy in the air.

The family didn't have a chance, they cried for help but no one would help, because of the amount of killers with high powered rifles shooting up the place. The gunmen blocked off the entrance of the road so that the police and fire brigade couldn't rescue the people in the house. It took some time before the emergency services arrived on the scene anyway, and by that time they were all dead burned bodies lying around in the burnt out house. The house had burglar bars over the windows and door. The gang killed the people by shooting, or cutting their throats. They weren't satisfied, so they locked the grill from outside so that no one could escape or get in to help save person or property. It was very disturbing to see relatives and friends mourning, but there was nothing they could have done to help.

Child killing was a favourite revenge of Jamaican gangs and gunmen. The death of the two babies was a signal to all Trinity's enemies that death was coming their way, and soon. Jamaican gangs liked to kill babies to show that they didn't have any mercy or sympathy when they were taking revenge. They could not allow a baby to grow up and take back revenge on their loved ones so that was why they killed babies and children. It was some years now since Trinity died, but he left a trail of destruction and death behind him. The policeman that asks Trinity if he wanted him to guard him was also accused of involvement in his death. That same corrupt cop is now a superintendent in the Jamaican police force.

Trinity's friends paid the police station where this cop worked a surprise visit, and they shot it up, killing two policemen. The other cop who was there when the corrupt cop offered Trinity protection, heard about what happened at the station and went into hiding. He was given a new identity and was never seen again. His house was burned down, and his two dogs were killed, but they never found him. The policeman's family were taken into protected custody because of the threats on their lives. In Kingston, two communities were put under curfew for two months. Trinity was dead and gone, but his friends were creating havoc. It was like Satan let loose on the world, and his enemies were shown no mercy in hell.

Cash was in place to deal with any eventualities, and the violence continued for almost a year before it cooled down. Even now, people are still fearful for their life. Don 'Wally', who ordered the killing of Trinity was gunned down in a New York night club with five of his body guards. Their bodies were sent to Jamaica for burial and on the day of Wally's funeral, there was a shooting involving a rival gang, and four mourners were killed. The worst part of it was when one of Trinity's friends went up to the coffin and shot the dead man in the forehead, and then spat in his face. While that was going on, people were running all over the cemetery dodging gun shots. The priest was crying out "shame on you" then one of the gunmen came up to him and said "shut your fucking mouth before you get what happened to that punk in the coffin."

The driver of the hearse and the workers were nowhere to be found to bury Wally. Some of the mourners ran out of their shoes, others ended up with broken hands and feet. There was this man and his wife who ran into a bush to hide, and was bitten by wasps. It was a joke to the cemetery workers because they remembered seeing the couple earlier on as two slim people attending the funeral. After being bitten by the wasps they were swollen and bloated. The Spanish Town police, with help from Kingston and the army, had to bury Wally because there was no one left in the cemetery to carry on with the funeral service. Even the brave priest ran, leaving his bible and sought refuge in a house nearby. The next day it was all over the news and in the newspapers, there were calls for the government to put security in place at all 'so-called dons' funerals.

From that day onward, all dons' funerals were heavily guarded by police and soldiers. The amount of gunshots that were fired at Wally's funeral could have supplied a small war or put a shooting range to shame. The police stated that they found over 10, 000 spent shells from AK47, M16, UZI and automatic pistols. The dead man's family entourage vehicles were shot up and set on fire. The ones who escaped had to hitch rides back home to Kingston. Two more people who attended the funeral were found two days later in a pond near the cemetery on a horse farm that is now a housing scheme runs by a don named Skendon, all drowned. The cemetery was located about 4-5 miles outside Spanish Town, and was one of the two cemeteries that the rich and famous buried their dead.

The Cemetery where the shooting incident took place was about three miles from where Trinity was born and grew up. All the dons who got killed in Jamaica and the US were buried at Dove Cot or Meadow Rest cemetery. Lots of people were left uneasy when Trinity got killed because they owed him money that he had loaned them. Pity they didn't know that he kept a diary of everything that happened in his life. Therefore, it wasn't hard for his family to find out all who owed him. Some went into hiding because they didn't want to repay the money they owed, often some got kidnapped, whilst some paid back their debts and were free to go about their business as usual. After Wally was killed, Trinity's friends took over all of his businesses and started to run things again in the US.

Wally talked rough, and was ruthless, but Trinity spoke soft and he was kind and gentle. Wally was the kind of guy who always killed his enemies and took over their businesses, while Trinity used economic sabotage to get hold of any businesses he wanted to control. Trinity would flood the market with 98% cocaine from Columbia at a cheap price, and that way he got control of the market; lots of people didn't like him for that. Wally didn't have the resources and contacts like Trinity, who was very good at business. It took some time for the shooting, killing, kidnapping and violence to cool off but everyone knew that it was just for a short while, the calm before the storm. Trinity's friends had solemnly vowed revenge, and they would stop at nothing until they killed all those involved in his death.

The government and the opposition came to an agreement to disassociate themselves from all dons, gunmen and violence even though; they were the ones who gave out the guns in Jamaica in the first place to hoodlums. The politicians only say that to fool the public but they are still friends with criminals. The police was used to killing many of the gunmen who the politicians could no longer control. Some of those gunmen were drugs dons who didn't take talk from anyone but some of them ran away to the States, UK, Canada and Europe during the crackdown. The government used some of their senior cops who operate death squads which specialised in extra-judiciary killings to hunt them down and murder them. Most of the dons who ran away returned as big businessmen, driving Lexus, BMW, Benz, Homer, F150, Escalade, Infinity, Bentley, Ferrari and other top of the range vehicles. These guys had become so powerful that they didn't take talk from the police or politicians seriously.

When Trinity was around no one bothered to run behind politicians asking for favours because Trinity was the big man and politicians were counted as nothing. Trinity wasn't the kind of guy who people could take for a fool, he could get anyone killed by the click of a finger, and he had the friends and support to dismantle threats. Things were getting out of hand, so the two political parties called a truce. Trinity supported the Jamaica Labour Party while Wally supported the People National Party. If things began to get out of hand, it would look like a full scale political war and the politicians didn't want that to happen. The violence died down for awhile and everything seemed to be back to normal.

The grave was as impressive as his many mansions that he died and left. People from all over the world came to look at Trinity's grave and to take pictures of it. It was like a tourist attraction in the community. Years passed after Trinity got murdered and his name still lived on like a legend to all who knew him. Despite all the millions and the friends he had, none of them could save his life. But his friends surely saw to it that his enemies were killed and his business empire restored. Trinity, with his movie star status was an icon to bad men all over Jamaica who wanted to go to 'foreign' to get rich quick. He would always told them that living in 'foreign' wasn't easy or 'a bed of roses', he told the guys that he went through hell to reach the top, and it only happened because he believed in himself and worked hard to reap success.

Spanner doing Community work

Spanner was the Chairman for the Barry & Lloyd Youth and Community Club and Trinity was going to help Spanner restore the Centre to its former glory, but unfortunately he got killed before that could happen. Barry & Lloyd was Spanner's pet project. After getting paroled from GP prison, Spanner returned back to Kitson Town to live. The centre was in a deplorable condition and there was no light, water, or doors on the building. Spanner got some youths together and they cleaned up the place, got the lighting installed, put zinc on the roof and put the doors and windows back on. Then Spanner took his three sewing machines to the centre where he started to teach the youths to sew their clothes. Spanner was instrumental in providing treats for the kids in and around Kitson Town annually.

He would hand out ice cream, school supplies, toys and provided bounce-about for the kids entertainment. Spanner was the one who introduced the British Save the Children Fund to Kitson Town so that the poor could get some help for their children. The politicians weren't interested so he had to do whatever he could to help. That was the kind of Don or area leader Spanner was. Kitson Town and Old Road was much better off when Spanner was around running the place. All the politicians did in Kitson Town was dividing the people which made the community worse off and stole the money that allocated for road repairs and for fixing the community centre.

Spanner was one of them who followed in Trinity footsteps but he wasn't as rich as Trinity in cash but Spanner was much luckier and maybe much wiser too. He went to the UK after Trinity died to seek a better life and he got caught up in some conspiracy theory and got nine years in Her Majesty Prison. Spanner was more intelligent but not that lucky as Trinity in monetary term because Trinity made lots of millions before he went to prison while Spanner made nothing.

It was two months after landing in England that he ended up in a conspiracy that sent him to prison for nine years. Spanner was wiser and always studying to get qualified in his chosen field. The reason for that is because he wanted to use whatever he learned to his advantage so that he could teach the youths in and around his community some of what he had learned. Spanner wasn't a selfish guy despite all the fight he got as a youth growing up in his community. One of the reasons why Spanner went to the UK was to help his family and his community. That's how much he loves humanity.

Trinity was a role model, maybe a bad one, but Spanner was more like a trend setter. He single handily took his three new expensive sewing machines to the community centre to teach the youths tailoring. He got no help from the government, MPs or councillor's but he did it and it inspired lots of youths to take up tailoring to earn a living. Because of what Spanner did, it inspired lots of young people from the community to be progressive. Some of the youths from Kitson Town are in America and the UK making use of the knowledge Spanner instilled in them.

Spanner used to link with the Social Development Commission and British Save the Children Fund in Spanish Town. He was instrumental in getting kids from Kitson Town to go on youth exchange programs in Canada and the UK. Through his help lots of parents got monetary help to send their kids to school. He was interested in getting rich by using his brain for the betterment of himself and his people. Nothing was wrong with that as long as he didn't steal or kill anyone to get rich.

The thing about Spanner was that he loved people, Trinity was a people person too but maybe not like Spanner who would go the extra mile to help his community. While Trinity would give away millions to people: cars, houses excreta, Spanner was more interested in doing things for the community that would make people better themselves and remembering him when he passed away. Spanners main interest was to work with the youths and build a community centre and deal with projects that would benefit the community and its people who lived in it. He took a few things out of Trinity's book, but he tweaked them with his own ideas. Spanner was at the General Penitentiary with Trinity and he was with him on the Friday before he got killed on that Sunday evening. It was three of them in the Land Rover discovery jeep on that Friday evening; Spanner, Trinity and his brother button.

Spanner warned the doctor about the Nigerian Scam

Bah, another brother of Trinity is now looking after the things that his brother dead and left. Spanner and Trinity's brothers and father got on well. Button married Spanner's cousin and they were all friends. Before Trinity's death he used to pick up Spanner at his work place, so one of the evenings Spanner introduced Trinity to two of his doctor friends. One of the doctors was Spanner's boss and the other was a good friend, both were in financial difficulties. On the Friday evening before Trinity left the office he promised to invest (US$250,000) in the IT firm that Spanner was working, but he died before the money was released. He loaned the other doctor (US$7,000) which was to be paid back to Spanner if anything happened to him. That (US$7, 000) was used to finance some Nigerian scam.

The Nigerian's were milking this doctor but he wouldn't listen to Spanner. Spanner went on the Internet where he printed out stuff for the doctor to see and learn about the Nigerian scam, even though they had already taken (US$ 85, 000) off him before. He was showed the evidence but he just wouldn't listen or believe. Spanner knew what was going on but this doctor was too simple, the Nigerian was taking him for a ride. Spanner told him that he was disgracing Jamaicans because no ghetto man would easily give up their hard earned cash like that. Moreover, Jamaicans liked to kill people who try to use them or take them for a fool. The Nigerians offered the doctor (US$30,000.000) if he helped them recover (US$100, 000.000) from the central bank of Nigeria. Spanner read some of the correspondences that they sent to the doctor, and couldn't understand how he allowed those people to tricked him. He was greedy and he lost all his businesses as a result of the Nigerian scam. He wants easy money so he lost his hard earned one.

They would ask him to send (US$3, 000, 5, 000 and 10, 000) to pay for Mr so and so to push through the paper work. Even though Spanner gave him the evidence as proof to show that the Nigerian were conning him, he didn't believe, so he ending up owing Trinity (US$7.000). When Trinity died, he thought that he was off and wouldn't have to pay back the money he borrows. Little did he know that, that the day before Trinity was killed, he told his brother about the money the Doctor owed him. It was Spanner duty to collect the money and the pressure was on him to prove himself as an enforcer. Spanner was told to use any means necessary to get back the money. This man was good to Spanner when Trinity was away, so he didn't want to kill him but he would have to repay back the money soon before Trinity brother ask someone else to collect it. That would discredit Spanner or undermines his don-ship, which would be a disgrace for him. Spanner couldn't afford for that to happen, so he had to act fast before someone take his place as the enforcer. If someone who doesn't know the Doctor should come to collect the money, it could be worst.

That would make it worst for the doctor because he was in financial difficulty and they would kill him. The money was only a loan and it was time to collect it but the doctor was playing games and it causes him and Spanner to fall out. He didn't want to repay back the money but he was playing with his life and time was running out. There was no violence going on at the time, but the pressure was on to collect all the money that was owed out to Trinity. Trinity brother didn't care about his death but he was more interested in his money. Spanner was a friend of Trinity's and his family and he didn't want the family to think that he wasn't interested in helping to get back the money owed to them. They were the executor of his estates so the money was technically theirs now. Spanner broke off friendship with the Doctor first because he was serious about collecting all the outstanding debt owed to Trinity.

Spanner went to one of the Doctor place of business and took out some equipment valued over a million dollars. That cause the doctor to call in the cops who contacted Spanner about the stuff he took. There were computers, fax machines, printers, copiers and lots of valuable tools that he used in his profession. The doctor was an eye doctor. The cops were onto Spanner so he released some of the stuff but kept some for himself. Spanner couldn't afford to get into anymore trouble with the law because he didn't have the cash to hire a top lawyer, nor did he have Trinity to bail him out. Jamaica was getting hot again so Spanner bought a ticket to London and ran away because he would have to kill some police or they kill him. The police was being paid by a woman politician who wanted Spanner dead so they were happy to used the doctor complaint as a disguise.

Spanner opinion

The police are corrupt and they participated in extra-judicial killing, and were immune from being punish or prosecuted for their crimes. The politicians are no better because they condoned with the wrong the police did. The police are supposed to serve, protect and reassure but instead they drive fear in the people. When cops got murdered everyone would say how brutal the gunmen are and how the killer should be punished. No one cares about when the police murdered an innocent man or child and get away with it. That's double standards at its best. Why doesn't the society call for the police and politicians to be punished for the crimes they committed? That will help to restore confidence and trust in the administration of law and justice for everyone no matter if that person is rich or poor in Jamaica. That kind of behaviour breeds contempt and distrust amongst the people in the ghettos. Hence the youths killed cops and didn't even care because society didn't care when the cop killed one of them. The majority of ghettos communities don't like cops or the rules of laws anyhow. There are so many scandal over the years with the politicians and all some of them do was to resign and later on they would get another job in politricks.

There is one law for the police, one for the politicians and the rich and one law for the poor. That caused citizens to hate the police and that's what helped to breeds crime. Trinity and all the ghetto dons before and after him saw the injustices that the government, police and the rich dished out to the poor. Jamaican police are armed to the teeth and every year lots of them got murdered and their guns got stolen. Jamaican gunmen don't respect police or the rule of the so-called law period. One of Trinity main argument was "why is it that police have to be armed to the teeth to go and get one gunman or don? After all it's only one person they want so one cop should be able to apprehend the gunman or don. Gangs, dons and gunmen all see police and politicians as sissies, bullies and wimp because they are all corrupt and cowards.

It was general knowledge that one gunman can take on a police station or division of cops alone. Police are coward and hence Trinity sanctioned lots of cop killing in the States and Jamaica. No ghetto people will trust the police or politicians until they stop dealing in corruption. Trinity was a law unto himself and people from all over respected him. Trinity asked "why is it that all movies that involve cops and bad guys, the cops always winning? In reality, in the ghettos gunmen took over police stations and killed some of the cops and most time they killed without getting caught. The fact of the matter was that the media is bias against the outlaws. The media should deal with reality hence I write this book to tell a true story, my story about the life of Trinity and Spanner as true Jamaican dons. These guys can teach about criminology.

It was in 1977 Trinity got his life sentence at the gun court and did most of his time at GP prison. Spanner first saw Trinity in 1982 after his last encounter in Kitson Town with the police and he left the area. The cops were out to kill him that day, and he never returned to Kitson Town until he left Jamaica. He went to America and got rich, and then he returned to Kitson Town, as the 'don of dons'. Trinity was the one who recognised Spanner in GP after seeing him with a group of new prisoners coming from the prison hospital. Trinity approached Spanner and asked if he was the little boy who lives at Pepper Granny house and Spanner told him yes. Not long after Trinity link up Spanner and gave him some cannabis (weed) to sell so that he could have money to buy whatever he needs.

Batty man, Gays, Chichi man, faggots- in GP

In those days in GP there were some serious batty man inside the prison, there was Ralph, Gingy Fly and a few more high profile faggots who literally runs the prison. Most of the senior wardens were faggots so those batty boys have the run of the prison. Lots of men goes into prison straight and came back out bow (gay) because they like their belly and love to smoke too much. These batty boys would seek out the prisoner who are weak and don't have anyone to visit them and give them stuff. In return they would have to give up their bottom as payment. Sometimes a guy would come into the prison slim and when it was time for them to go home they came out the prison fat. No one knows what those batty boys were doing to those guys for them to be getting fat.

There was this warden who runs the kitchen in GP who was a batty man. Most batty men work in the prison and they control the food that they sell the prisoners who cook their own food. Lots of bad men say they hate batty man but when they go to prison, it's the batty men who cook their food and they have to deal with batty man some way or another. There was this dumb man working in the kitchen but he wasn't gay, one morning early he enters the kitchen and saw the warden having sex with a prisoner. He was furious and he run and grabs the screw and lifts him off the floor and ran towards the copper to dump in it. A copper is this huge thing that the food is cook in, it was a big pot almost like a 44 gallon drum.

The warden was lucky that another warden came to the kitchen that morning and he beg the prisoner not to kill the batty man warden. After the dumb prisoner put him down, he ran out the kitchen with his pant down his ankle. As for the prisoner who was getting the fuck, the warden that save the comrade blew his whistle and wardens from all over the prison came running toward the kitchen. They beat the batty boy prisoner until he couldn't move; a few days later he died in the Kingston Public Hospital from his injuries. Nothing happen to the warden and it was business as usual in the prison. Not long after Ralph got released and he couldn't manage the freedom so he rape a man, his wife and the son to return back to prison.

Spanner in London

When Spanner went to the UK, he stayed with some friends in Hackney on Median Road near Homerton Hospital. They were some people he knew while living in Water House in Kingston 11, and some from Kitson Town where he grew up and lived before migrating. Spanner came to the UK to live, study and better himself. At no time was Spanner thinking of getting involved in drugs dealing. The house that he was living in was used as a base but at no time was there any drugs in the house.

Spanner spent two months in Hackney with the people who picked him up at Heathrow airport. One night about 8.pm, Spanner went out to buy some drinks at the off licence (liquor store) on lower Clapton Road, when four white guys in their thirties jumped him. He thought they were criminals but they later identified themselves as police. They searched him, took down his details and told him that they were watching the address. They even told Spanner about Trinity who had been killed a few months earlier in Jamaica. Spanner wasn't doing anything wrong; he had just come from Jamaica to live in the UK. He had nothing to worry about, but little did he know that the police were out to get him too as part of the gang.

Spanner's girlfriend had just come from the US to visit him in the UK, it was her first visit to London and they stayed at 73 Chatsworth Road in Hackney. She was staying for two weeks, but the visit only lasted for ten days. One morning at about 7.am, eight policemen came knocking on Spanner's door. First, he thought they were criminals because of the way they dressed and looking like some drugs addict. He looks through the peep hole, he then opened the door after they showed him the warrant and police badges and he let them in. They looked like a bunch of drugs dealers and crack head that were sleeping rough. His girlfriend was naked on the bed because he had just finished giving her his morning ride (making love to her).

After the police finished searching, they found a coat with £472 in it which they took away and the court confiscated it after the trial. The cops were slightly disappointed that they didn't get Spanner and

Shangul on the murder which they knew was ordered on behalf of Trinity's death. While at Stoke Newington police station Spanner's American girlfriend had to cut short her vacation and return to the States. At Pentonville prison Spanner met Power one of Trinity friends who was one of his hit man. He was inside for murdering one of Trinity enemy, but after a few months, he was out and continued killing for the revenge of his friend's death. Trinity was the one who paid the wardens (screws) at Spanish Town prison to let Power escape from his life sentence that he was serving. He escaped with their help and ended up in Britain. Power was wanted in Jamaica, but he was in the UK killing and robbing drugs dons on behalf of Barney.

Spanner loved sex and he was the kind of guy who would make love up to eight times a night. Spanner woke up early and had sex so it was his second time for that morning and he was sure he got his American girlfriend pregnant. The cops didn't care about the naked woman, so they searched the flat, took the money that was in the flat, jewellery and any paperwork they could find, to implicate him in the conspiracy case they were investigating. On that same morning, the cops cornered Shangul with another guy at a petrol station on Homerton High Street in East London. There were lots of police from SO19 with guns and they surrounded the car that he was travelling in and they broke the windows and took Shangul out. They arrested Shangul and took him to Stoke Newington police station where they interviewed him and Spanner.

At the station they questioned Spanner about a murder that took place at Powerscroft Road a week after he landed in Britain. They were also looking for a guy they called 'Barney' who Spanner knew, and he was also the head of Trinity's business in the UK. They searched the flat and Spanner but they didn't find any drugs or gun. They only found some money and details that they would used in the trial to convict Spanner on conspiracy to supply class "A" drugs a year later in Southwark Crown Court. He was tried and convicted by a bunch of white, racist jurors, prosecutor and judge because he was black and from Jamaica.

Before being sentence Spanner and Shangul were taken to Pentonville prison where they spent two months before being transferred to Brixton prison. Two months later, after going to Bow Street Magistrate Court, the case was transferred to Southwark Crown Court. After going to court for a year and two retrials, Spanner and Shangul were found guilty and were given 9 years sentence. One of the cop told Spanner before he got sentence that if he didn't co-operate with them in solving the murder of Shaggy, then they would let him get a big bird, which was what happened after the trial. In the trial, the judge and jurors were all white, which made Spanner mad. He told the judge that they were all racist and that once a person was black and from Jamaica, they were branded as murderer and drug dealers, which was unfair.

The court couldn't find Spanner guilty in the first trial because the jurors were mixed and the jurors couldn't come to a decision. It was only after they got information from Jamaica that Spanner had been to prison there, they used it in the retrial to get a conviction. The British cops sent to Jamaica to investigate Spanner and the Jamaican cops were happy like a 'puppy dog' to give information that Spanner went to prison in the 1980s, for manslaughter. That was what the British cops wanted and they used it to get a retrial to convict Spanner which was bad because he felt the Jamaican authorities had betrayed him. The court stated that Spanner should have told them about the conviction in Jamaica, and because he didn't tell the jury they should discard everything he had said in the first trial, as a lie. That made Spanner even madder.

Spanner asked the judge "how could I tell the police or court that I went to prison in Jamaica when I was in my teens and it has no relevance to this trial? A matter of fact it's none of the UK business. I was charged for conspiracy, so what bearing does it have in this case?" before the verdict the judge told the juror to disregard the earlier evidence. Spanner was very upset but there was nothing he could do, he was like a lamb to the slaughter. That's how justice in the British court system worked.

Spanner knew that the court was against anything Jamaican, so he told the court that he went to prison before the prosecutor could reveal the information. Spanner told the court: "In my country it is law to put up a sign on your property marked 'trespasser will be prosecuted' which is on our family land. My mother had lots of land in Jamaica and if I should see you the judge, prosecutor or the police on my land, I would have the right to shoot you without asking any questions" Spanner knew that he was going down, but he was going with his gun blazing. Spanner continued: "lots of judges, prosecutors, senior police and politicians are paedophiles which are disgusting and a more serious crime than conspiracy to selling drugs. Today as I am standing in the court, who knows if the judge, prosecutor, police and some of the juror isn't paedophiles? So who are you to judge me because of my past and colour?"

The judge told the juror not to take into account what Spanner had said earlier, everyone knew they did, and they found him guilty within 40 minutes. The judge said "stand up please; today I am going to sentence you both for conspiracy. I am taking into account your age, which are 37 and 38 respectively, I am giving you both 9 years in prison which will be hard for you in a foreign land. You will have to do half the time and should be paroled after doing four and a half years". They were taken out the courtroom to their cells to wait for the Serco Security van to transport them back to prison. The police didn't get anyone for the murder, but they were ok with the sentence that Spanner and Shangul got.

Five years later after Spanner finished his time in prison; he was transferred to Colnbrook Immigration Detention Centre (The British equivalent to the Nazi concentration camp) where he spent two years before being released. The UK government ordered his deportation back to Jamaica because they think he was too dangerous to roam the street of Britain. Shangul got deported a few months later and send straight to prison, not long after three prisoners got murdered. The war started again.

Two of the cops who were involved in Power's case when he got life sentence before he ran away from Jamaica, got murdered in Rema, West Kingston, on Water Street. While investigating the murder of four men who were accused of collaborating with Cow, who robbed Trinity in America while coming from Mexico with a consignment of cocaine and left him for dead in the desert. Spanner response was "It's not uncommon for police to get murdered and their guns got taken away by bad boys" Trinity's friends knew that British and Americans along with other foreign agents were operating in Jamaica but they didn't care. After all Jamaica was their country and they could kill whoever they please without worrying. They knew that they could pay a cop to destroy the evidence or get information on the person who made the report.

The guys were calling for agents and cops to identify themselves so that they could kill them and return their body to their respective embassies in body bags. They were keen to identify the cops and agents families which would be a bonus. Trinity always despised foreign cops working in Jamaica, and all dons would have been glad to kill spies. Spanner asked "how could the Jamaican government be so stupid to let this former British cop to setup office in Jamaica? The guy must have being selling information to the British and American from 2004; he must be seen as an enemy of the State. He was a spy"

These foreign agents and cops managed to ruin lots of Jamaican lives and send many innocent people to prison, amounting to hundreds of years. Take for instance Trinity's friends City Puss, who killed two DEA agents in California, on the boss order after they destroyed a shipment of his drugs. When Trinity died, he left a manual on how to deal with the DEA, FBI, Interpol and other foreign government agents. He was a professional who knew the in, and out of all these agencies. Jamaican cops were like a target because at least two would get killed each month. The cops, in return, would kill twenty gunmen in questionable circumstances. No matter how many bad boy the cops killed, killing two cops for the months was more valuable to the underworld.

Trinity's death caused lots of people killed and some ended up in prison because of their involvement in the murder spree that followed. From the day Trinity got murdered in October 2001 over (100) cops got killed because of their criminal involvement. If a cop killed one gunman they had to expect a few of them to get killed also. It was a dog eat dog world out there in Jamaica. When Trinity was alive, loads of cash was around because he had lots of construction work going on all over the island. There were many spin offs and benefit from all the activities, to the wider economy, from the taxi man, to the shopkeeper in rural Jamaica. Spanner and Trinity were 100% Jamaican in all their dealings and beliefs. The guys just loved their country.

The deportation of Spanner back to Jamaica

Spanner was the only one who could calm down the killing that was going on all over Jamaica because of Trinity's death. He didn't like what was going on and it was time to stop all the madness, but first he would have to be free from detention in the UK. On the day of

Spanner's release from immigration detention in the UK, he touched down in Jamaica, at Kingston, Norman Manley International airport where a crowd of people greeted him. The people were happy to see Spanner. He was really delighted of the professional service he received on Jamaica love bird.

Spanner returned on an Air Jamaica flight to a hero's welcome! Spanner said to the cheering crowds "friends and well wishers, it's so nice to be back in my own country where I am welcome. In the UK black people have no say and are victims of institutional racism. Because of who I am and the colour of my skin, I was sent to prison for nine years on false allegations. As you can see, I am now free; I will dedicate my time to uplifting my community and its people". There were cheers from everyone and the noise was deafening. Spanner continued "my main aim now is to forget about Britain and its racist policies and help to rebuild my country by investing in it. Trinity died and didn't get to finish his mission. I will have to accomplish my goal by giving young people the opportunity to choose a career other than crime"

"To do that I would have to remove a few stumbling blocks out of the way, because I don't want anyone to trip over them and get hurt, like Trinity. My aim is to give Kitson Town and all the communities around it, especially Old Road District where I grew up a first class community centre with all the modern technology. Education is the key to help unlocking the crime situation in Jamaica and I want to be remembered for the good I do. The government aren't doing anything for poor people, and fighting crime is not their main priority. Where is the large sum of money that they got from foreign governments to help the poor go? No wonder dons like Milo, Jack man and Bulby of Spanish Town, Dudus from Tivoli, Bang from Samakan, Zekes from Matthews Lane, Rikey Boo & Scandal from Water House, and Joel from Papine, George Flash, Starky, Shabba and many more dons from Kingston and across Jamaica, who have to filled the gap where government failed".

Spanner "I would love to see more productive Jamaicans, like Trinity but not as an international drugs king pin share their knowledge with the youths. Educationally and in business I would love to see ghetto youths excel and take advantage of all opportunities present to them". Spanner was free and back in Jamaica and his first job, as Trinity's friend, was to call for peace and no more killing. Spanner said "we want unity within the various communities and that was his aim".

The death of Spanner Grandmother

Spanner loved his granny, world without end, and until today day he is still upset over her death. He wanted to treat her like the Queen she was before she died as a way of saying 'thank you granny' but she died while he too was in GP prison without anyone telling him. The family knew that Spanner loved his grandmother and if he should get that news while in prison he would surely escape. They didn't want that to happen, so they asked everyone who worked inside the prison who knew Spanner, not to tell him. It was three years after his grandmother died, he left the General Penitentiary. It was when he went to look for his sick grandmother that he found out that she had died. He was upset but there was nothing he could do to get her back, so he vowed to make himself a man and his duty was to tomb her with a nice head stone on her grave.

Usain Bolt

Spanner said "what I want these foreign people to do is try to get to know the true Jamaican people and their culture". A very good example to compare would be ***Usain Bolt***, he is from rural Jamaica and he is not involved in crime. He is one of the best things that could ever happen to Jamaica, he won three gold medals in the Olympics in China and he made Jamaicans and the world proud. There are good and bad things in every country but what Bolt did can and should be used as a starting to unify the nation. The youth is a role model to the young people of Jamaica and the world and he shows that hard work and dedication can bear fruit.

Spanner used another example: "look at what Trinity, a country boys from rural Jamaica, who went to America and look what he had achieved? He showed that Jamaican are resourceful and can be whatever they wanted to be. He was a drugs don but he was a very successful one.

The Jamaica Diaspora

It is time the Jamaica Diaspora stand up and be counted in the development of Jamaica. They should not allow themselves to be bias or even support corrupt politicians and any government that doesn't look after its citizens. These people are influential and should put pressure on the government to clean up their act.

Spanner Reflecting on Jamaica achievement and unfair treatment

Trinity became one of the richest drug dons to ever come out of Jamaica and he was very good at what he did, like Bill Gate and computers, that's how good the guy was in drugs running". Trinity and Spanner were always upset when they heard the foreign news press saying bad things about Jamaica. Spanner would say "no one mentions a thing about the many Jamaica Teachers, Nurses, Engineers, Doctors, Athletes, Musicians and many more professionals who are in the UK and North America, in fact all over the world working for the betterment of mankind. It hurt to see Jamaica being treated unfairly by foreign governments and the press. Jamaicans rebel against injustice and the rebelliousness is in our blood and reggae land people don't like injustices and being push around".

Spanner mentioned whenever Jamaicans were in front of the UK and US court dem never get a fair trial because the judges were racist and bias. Trinity spoke out against the treatment of MI5, CIA, US and UK courts and the press who were racist and bias against Jamaicans. He would say that foreign agents stitched up Jamaicans all the time and gave the country a bad name. Spanner loved his country but hated the politicians who were oppressing the poor. He liked to present himself as an ambassador for 'Jam Rock' He encourage many foreigner to visit Jamaica and he always defends Jamaica when anyone speak bad about the country.

Les Green a Scottish policeman worked in Jamaica, the Scottish were the main culprits who enslaved Jamaicans but what he said about corrupt cops is the truth. About corruption, Les Green was in a very good position to talk about corrupt cops. Lots of policemen who got murdered were corrupt for real. The only people who mourned them were the police force and their family. Because of the police force corrupt ways, no one mourn or misses them when they got killed. Sad but true.

The Death of Spanner's Brother

He knew the danger of drugs because he saw what it did to his brother Paul, who was killed in Spanish Town. Spanner got the news that his brother was killed by a gang in revenge because they couldn't catch him. Paul was chopped to death. He was minced up like minced meat. They knew that Paul was Spanner's brother, he had always warned his brother and told him to stop using crack but he wouldn't listen so he ended up getting killed. Spanner loved his brother and he had to act after they killed his brother.

Jamaican Politics

Spanner and Trinity were political activists before they become dons. They knew that all politicians were corrupt so it wasn't a surprising to see the people abandoning politics to be on Trinity's winning team. Trinity was giving people work, while politicians were robbing the poor and killing off the people who were getting wise. Trinity was the man of the moment and even the politician would visit Old Road to see what this guy was doing. The roads were bad and desperately in need repair, but politicians didn't care about fixing them but Trinity was making plans to asphalt all the roads in his community.

Spanner was in politics when his eyes were at his knees, meaning that he went into politics at a young age. He was involved in politics in Jamaica from he was about 9 years old. Dah was Spanner's granny and a Jamaica Labour Party member and supporter before he was born. Spanner grew up seeing his grandmother go to political meetings and conferences at the national arena every year. When that guy talked about the corruption in Jamaican politics, you had to believe and listen to him.

Spanner worked with many care takers, MPs and Councillors for the two major parties and the lesser one which is the National Democratic Movement. Because of all the corruption he saw at one stage he got fed up and switched to the NDM. The guy loved politics and the buzz that went with it. He once told that politics was the best entertainment because, as an activist you can play a major role in everything that happens in a constituency and the outcome of an election.

An activist may collect extortion from any business within the constituency boundary. After an election or before it starts are when the extortion really kicks in. Businesses will never get away from the extortion racket that takes over the country. Some of these businesses gave money to buy gunshots and other illegal activities to help make the candidates they support win. Some of the business owners also have ulterior motives. Some have ambitions to becoming councillor and maybe one day caretakers then MP. With the help of gunmen, thugs and extortionists these businesses gave out money to activists, even after the election, for protection. When the time come for selection of candidates in the constituency, that was the time you would see some of these so-called 'financiers' step forward.

The businessmen and women had already established themselves, so going through the process of selection would received no objection when the time came for them to run as an MP or Councillor. Spanner sometimes opposed the selection of some of those so-called business or community leaders from being selected as political representatives in West Central St Catherine. When dons or gunmen put a politician in power, those politicians had to do things to suit the thugs.

That was not good for Jamaican politics or the country, but that was the way things worked. Spanner was fed up with the way things were going in West Central St Catherine and across Jamaica, but he alone couldn't stop it. That was why he switched so many times to see if he could find someone in the party's that really cared for the people. The politicians would bribe the people with money, and they would forget about the many problems that face them.

The businessmen and women had already established themselves through bribery and hooliganism, so going through the process of selection would be receive with no objection. When gunmen put in a politician in power that politician have to do things to suit the thugs who help him to win. That is not good for Jamaican politics but that was the way things worked. Spanner was fed up with the ways things was going in West Central St. Catherine but he alone couldn't stop it. That was why he switched so many times to see it he could find someone and the party that really cared for the people. Sadly he was always sabotaged by the same people who he was fighting for. The politicians would give out JA$500, one politician even gave out rotten chicken back to her constituency and school things, but Spanner couldn't afford to give to the people those incentives so the corrupt politicians always won. All these things corrupted the constituencies because most of the people were poor and in need of financial help.

It's a disgrace to see how the politicians treated the voters with contempt. There was this woman caretaker from the People National Party who got over 5 tons of outdated chicken backs from off the wharf that was destine for the Riverton dump, but she distributed it all over West Central St. Catherine in 1997, during the election campaign. The chicken back wasn't fit for human consumption, but she still gave it out as a way of buying votes and she won and for five years she did nothing for her constituency.

Spanner and Sheriff was sparring partner during the politics and were responsible for distributing some of the stale meat that wasn't fit to eat. After they found out that the meat was rotten they dumped the van load of rotten meat in a bush up by Top Mountain, but this caretaker wasn't having any of it. They were order to go and pick up back the meat so that someone else could distribute it. Spanner and Sheriff voiced their concerns and opposition but other activists carried news on them and they were sidelined. The meat was collected from where it was dumped and was distributed. Someone should have gone to prison for that disgraceful behaviour.

This politician, asked her politician friend to sent his police death squad to oversee the running of the constituency to keep Spanner and Sheriff quiet. This same security minister from the P.N.P was also the main defence for all the top PNP criminals, gunmen, murderers and extortionist party supporters. The woman became MP and don't ask if she didn't sabotage Spanner, Sheriff and all the other activists who opposed her ways of running the constituency. Spanner and Sheriff were blacklisted.

It was a disgrace to see how the General Secretary of the P.N.P, who was a woman, along with the security minister, fought their fellow PNP caretaker Mr Blake. This guy Mr Blake was the Caretaker who the people wanted, but the P.N.P decided that they wanted their friend in the seat. So headquarters sent in their goons, along with lots of corrupt cops from Kingston, to keep away Spanner, Sheriff and all those who opposed the selection of the woman, she got selected and Mr Blake was pushed out of his own party.

That's the reality of Jamaican politics. The thing that was most worrying was the seal of approval Jamaica's corrupt government got from other foreign countries. Spanner said "I remember when the leadership race was going on for the People National Party, and the way how they fight against Miss Portia Simpson from becoming the true leader and put in a former prime minister who later step down. All those things I saw with my eyes and saw that Jamaican politicians were criminals who needed to be stopped, and perhaps let the church be put in charge of the country.

There was this guy who was the junior foreign affair minister in the Prime minister office, as his reward to help stopping Portia from being the Prime Minister. He came to Kitson Town and Spanner talked to him and he told Spanner that the party don't want Portia to lead because she was going to bring in too many of her old comrade friends. Spanner asked "what was he talking about and he said that Dr D.K Duncan would be involved in the party and they didn't want that.

These things happened to let Spanner realise how corrupted politicians was in Jamaica. Spanner though he knew all the politicians who gave out guns and stole ballot boxes to win their seat in Parliament. There was even a former Governor General who tried to murder his opponent in the 1980 general election campaign in St. James while running for a seat for the P.N.P. He tried to kill the J.L.P candidate who happens to be the foreign affair minister in the Bruce Golding government and it was only God on that man's side or else he would be killed. That MP later became the minister of health in the 1980s in the Seaga government. Spanner "I don't even like to talk about the wrongs I have see done by politicians and the police".

There was this one incident when Spanner handed over a gun to a policeman to take to the station and the same policeman's took the gun and gave it to his drugs dealer friends to guard his crack house, in front of Olympic Garden station. Spanner didn't trust most police in Jamaica; he thought some of them wanted to kill him because of what he knew. Rumours had it that a politician had tried to get Spanner killed by police and thugs from Matthews Lane in Kingston.

It should be noted that Bruce Golding grew up in a little district name Saint Faith in St Catherine as a J.L.P because his dad was an MP in the Jamaica Labour Party. A school was named after Bruce late father Tacius Golding. At one stage Bruce was so fed up of the corrupt politics he was involved in that he switched to become the head of the National Democratic Movement. He switched back again to the JLP after being in the wilderness for a few years, he became the leader, and led the party to victory in the 2007, general election. Bruce became the Prime Minister of Jamaica and rewarded the gang of five MPs who Seaga once banished from the party, at one stage the gang of five were told to sing a "Sankie' and find their way back home.

Spanner said "I remember after the 1972 general election which the young Michael Manley won by a land slide. He and his cousin Mabrak, Billy Gentles and Dicky the driver of Ms Enid Bennett blue VW van went around distributing food to J.L.P supporters. Spanner was only nine at the time and he took an interest in politics. That was often a way of buying votes, using food that was donated by other foreign governments, to the poor people of Jamaica. Sad to say but these thing still happen in the way of scarce resources for party patronage. Spanner said "before he left Jamaica he got a voucher to collect zincs and other housing materials for his house, he left the voucher with his kid's mother to collect the things but she didn't get them. Some other person did collect the good and it have to be in collaboration with the politician who gave out the voucher".

Spanner was only nine when he began to take an interest in politics, so it wasn't a surprise to most people who knew him when he became a chief political tactician in his party in West Central St Catherine. Spanner remained an honest and loyal character in politics while helping the people and not himself. He likes to help people but what the politicians did was to fool and steal from the people to fill their pocket and send their kids to the best school in America and UK. From that early age Spanner took up politics until today because he likes to help people but what the politician does is to fool and steal from the people.

Ms Bennett was the MP for a very long time in West Central St Catherine. She represented the Jamaica Labour Party for 32 years before she bowed out of 'Politricks' but she could have done better for West Central St. Catherine. Most of the constituency is remained without water, good roads, training centres, factories and community centres. Spanner was too young to know what took place before 1972, but he was told that the J.L.P was in power and the prime minister was Hugh Larson Sharer. He took over after Prime Minister Donald Sangster was killed or committed suicide?

It wasn't until 1980 that Spanner actually got involved in the heart of politicking as a 17 year old J.L.P supporter, who still couldn't vote. He campaigned all over West Central St. Catherine as a Labourite for his party. During the 1980s people from all over the country called him deliverance. Spanner was known across Jamaica as a J.L.P supporter and activist by the time the general election was called. The 1980s election campaign was very intense and lots of people got killed because of the parties they supported. Mr Manley was a good Prime Minister, but the capitalists who were in charge of the resources sabotaged his policies to fill their own pockets from the black market with imported goods. If the Jamaican people had listened to Manley, and taken up his offer to produce what they eat and for export; the country would be in a better place today.

Spanner said "I remembered the incident with the J.L.P candidate, from Browns Hall, when a certain senior P.N.P Member of Parliament in the Manley government was involved in a shooting that left a J.L.P supporter dead. This MP was accused of using a M16 rifle to kill and intimidate the opposition Jamaica Labour Party supporters. During the 1972-80 general elections, stealing ballot boxes in West Central St. Catherine and other part of the country was the norm. The J.L.P and P.N.P stole ballot boxes to ensure their candidates won the elections, a disgraceful act to democracy. That practice still exists in all garrison constituencies in Jamaica today. I don't know how the politicians who represented garrison constituencies sleep at night knowing that they won with stolen votes. How can a person get 110% vote in an election when one can only get 100%?

Spanner wasn't involved in the stealing of the ballot boxes, but he was an integral part in the intimidating processes to gain vote for his party. George Bush senior, was the head of the CIA at the time and the US was in favour of the Jamaica Labour Party to form the next government. The election campaign was a vicious one with the CIA and America on the J.L.P side while Cuba and Castro were on the P.N.P side. There were PNP supporters who went to Cuba to train as militant fighters. The guys, who went to Cuba, were well trained in using their M16 and AK47 rifles. There was a guy by the name of Bang who was involved in one of the 'Wailer's' musician murder, he was like a musician playing his instrument when he fired his M16 rifle in Water House, he too went to Cuba. The Manley government was sabotage by Bush and Spanner Jamaica Labour Party won.

Because of the CIA and the JLP sabotaging tactic, there was no food during the 1980s election and the Jamaican people couldn't get flour, rice, cornmeal to buy and salt fish to put in their Ackee. Jamaican didn't like banana flour but it was the only flour that was available. People had to cook Ackee and eat it with tinned mackerel or chicken back. That was when the Jamaican term 'tun yuh hand and mek fashion' really worked. People were cooking callaloo with Ackee as substitute for (salt-ting) vegetable to eat with their food. Even Kerosene oil was short and the poor were sleeping in the dark. The food shortages were a plot to get the J.L.P in power. Edward Seaga was like a hurricane, and he used the food shortage as his election campaign weapon. That was to show the world the kind of politics the politicians used in Jamaica to win their seats in parliament.

Over 800 people lost their lives because of politics which was a disgrace on Jamaica political leaders. On the night of the election the J.L.P won. America was happy, because they claimed that they helped rescue Jamaica from communist Cuba which wasn't true. Cuba treated Jamaica better than the US. The Cubans gave Jamaica three nice schools, what did the US give us? A steady shipment of cocaine and all manner of evil that followed where ever America goes.

To everyone surprise, within a few days after the election all shops and supermarkets were well stocked with all the products that were previously so scarce, during the election. Only the blind couldn't see what was happening. There were no ships in or out of Jamaica during the food shortage, so where the food did came from? From that day onward Spanner found out the root and branches of corruption in Jamaica political system and it makes him sick to the stomach. He felt ashamed of Jamaica politicians because of the way they were openly corrupt.

In Jamaica many MPs are directors of company that they owned. Some even run businesses that their friends give government contracts. To take up their MP post they had to resign. This is one of the ways where the corruption came into play. Some of those MPs would be given ministerial post and they would use their position to give out contracts to their family and their friends who were in charge of their companies. If they don't own a company, they have friends who do and some of them collect two kinds of kick backs money. They would collect for awarding the contract and out of the profit made from the work done. Spanner said "there are so many ways to beat the system, I had seen it all. Some of the MPs are solicitors, businessmen/women and if they aren't, they have friends who are, so it's easy to beat the system. While others who knew what's going on will turn blind eyes to protect their friends".

Most big businesses evade paying stamp duties because they have people at the wharf to release the goods without paying taxes for it. If and when they get caught, they don't go to prison because they have friends in high places. Some big businesses even steal electricity to run their businesses, how disgraceful is that? Bonded warehouses are the main culprit, the owners of those properties and businesses are presuming to be outstanding citizens, but they sometimes are the biggest crooks. Spanner said "I have many custom officers' friends who released good at the wharf for a fraction of the cost".

Most Jamaican knew someone in high office who is corrupt. Spanner said "I could give names of politicians, police, JP, examiners, custom officers, official at the passport office, birth papers office, and tax office who are all corrupt. Those people break the law every day and in return it hurts the country economy. Three quarter of all Jamaican drivers have to buy their license, that's a fact. I can get birth papers and passports for any nationals to show that they are Jamaican. How sad is that, maybe one of those person could be a terrorist?"

To measure the scale of corruption by public officials, just look at the cars they drive and the houses some of them got. Police don't get much pay but some of them have the biggest houses and flashiest cars. I am not saying that all police are criminals. Spanner continued "I don't know how those custom officers sleep well at night knowing that they cleared the guns for the criminals knowing that the same guns are what killing Jamaicans. As for the police who sell criminals guns, shame on them, they are contributing to the murders and destruction of Jamaica. Mr and Mrs Politicians you're not innocent because you shouldn't have encouraged violence in politics. Giving out guns to win election seats was wrong and disgraceful and now Jamaica reaps what you all had sow which is murder and mayhem.

Portia Simpson was running for the presidency for the People National Party which she should have won but they sabotaged her, people from P.N.P headquarters came to Kitson Town to persuade people from voting for Mr Blake or Ms Simpson. Blake was supporting

Ms Simpson and not P.J Patterson but Patterson ended up winning and consequently became the prime minister. That set back Ms Simpson for years, but Patterson resigned, and she became the first women prime minister for Jamaica. The things that hurt most were that the infighting was coming from people who represented the P.N.P, and called themselves comrades.

During the 1980s lots of M16, Ak47 rifles and hand guns made it into the hands of criminals through the two political parties. There was this famous shipment of guns from the US by the CIA for the J.L.P to fight the communist supporting P.N.P. The Manley government was seen as a threat to the US and there were also lots of Cuban all over Jamaica at that time. The Cubans were working in the construction sector, building schools and houses. The opposition didn't like the way Manley was friendly with Castro so they went around preaching that communism was taking over Jamaica.

The P.N.P did have its fair share of AK47 rifles and many hand guns to fight a war. It was war on the Jamaican people by the two political parties to get their vote which left death and destruction behind. It was that shipment of guns that was destined for one party but was hijack by the other which was the deciding factor on who had the most power, and could killed the most people. The JLP lost a few of their dons but they were victorious at the poll.

Having more guns meant more power and that was exactly what happened in 1980s because the party with the most guns won. That caused lots of high powered rifles to be in the hands of more criminals who were using them to kill their fellow Jamaicans. It was ironic that not one of those politicians ever got kill by the guns that they bought and distributed to criminals. Maybe not so far from now, we will see politicians being murder and I guarantee that that is the time they are going to take stock and set things right. Jamaica has too many natural resources that the country could top in and help to ease the joblessness. Creation of jobs is what the people want and an end to the crime situation.

Spanner asked "I just want to know how politicians sleep at night knowing that they helped to make Jamaica what it is today, a lawless country that is full of corruption and murderers?" Spanner detested politician who gives their supporters guns to kill their countrymen. This is what Spanner would sometimes say "when I see the hypocrites on television or in parliament my heart bleeds. Blood is on their hands and they seem not to care or bother because they think that they are untouchable".

Being in parliament gave Jamaican politicians' immunity from prosecution and prison, none of the other politicians on either side wanted change to that system because they all cover for each others. Most of the Jamaican politicians are corrupt and should be put on the firing squad. Spanner was on three sides of Jamaican politics. The best option would be the National Democratic Movement who didn't give out any guns to control garrison constituencies or support the use of violence.

The bad thing about the NDM was that some of its officers were former JLP or PNP officers; therefore, there was always the possibility of having bad eggs in the group. Apart from Patterson and Sangster it was assumed that all other Prime Ministers were associated with notorious killers. Spanner "I am not going to call anymore names, but I happen to knew all about all the criminals who were enforcer for past and present PM and other politicians. Sad but true".

In 1990 Spanner switched from the J.L.P, which he had officially supported for many decades, to the P.N.P. After they removed Mr Blake, Spanner and his friend Sheriff became the right hand men for the P.N.P candidate Mr Dewdney, a director at Jamaica Boilers Limited at the time. The candidate was living in the area in a district named Paul Mountain and was known to most people. Spanner and some of his friends put their support behind Mr Dewdney as a revolt to get out the J.L.P Member of Parliament Ms Enid Bennett, but she won the election by 250 votes.

Mr Dewdney came on the scene too late to run a good campaign, so he lost and gave up his caretaker role a few weeks later to Keste Miller another PNP caretaker. Spanner was the one who took Mr Miller around the constituency to meet the delegates and area leaders. Mr Miller was only holding the seat until the P.N.P found someone suitable. There was this other Lawyer by the name of Linton Walters who came on the scene after lawyer Miller had left, who was interested in getting the caretaker role and Spanner used to take him around but after a time he lost interest. He is now general secretary of the PNP.

So the new caretaker was that woman, who disrespected the whole of West Central St. Catherine voters, by giving out spoils chicken back to the people in return for their vote. The people were so foolish that they voted her in as a MP. Spanner, Sheriff and many more area leaders worked with her for a short time before they found out that she wasn't good for the constituency and withdrawn their services and support. It was too late for everyone else to withdraw their support because most of the other area leaders had already campaigned for her and got everyone to vote for her.

By the time Spanner found out the character of the woman and started campaigning against her, she was already trough the gate. She had won, and used the police to keep Spanner and the rest who disapproved of her quiet. She was an unpopular MP, and she only served one term before the people voted her out of office. After Spanner fall out with that woman, he returned back to the J.L.P to support the new candidate, Dr Kenneth Baugh. The Doctor came on the scene too late after Enid Bennett resigned. If he did come on the scene a bit earlier that Barker couldn't win by the small margin. Anyway The Doctor and Spanner continued to work hard in the constituency for the next couple of years before the next election.

Everyone was fed up after the defeat of the J.L.P candidate 'The Doctor' who remained a hard working and caring caretaker. Or was he up to no good like the others? Most MPs pretend to be caring and hard working during an election campaign or after they lost, but when they won they tend to forget their constituency. No one wanted to bother with politic, so Spanner asked Morgie to run as the councillor for the Red Hill division, which he accepted. Starkey and the rest of area leaders didn't want Morgan to be their councillor so they withdraw their support. Spanner and Morgan son decided to help him to become the councillor so they start to campaign on his behalf. During the campaign Jen was representing the PNP. But she lost

Every day they went to different places in the constituency giving out goodies to get people on board. To get Starkey on board Morgie have to bribe him with JA$20,000. Spanner and Jacky went out every day until Morgie was nominated for the councillor role, which he later won as a Councillor. However, Morgie didn't honour his pledge to Spanner and his son. That's what happened in Jamaica's politics, after an election, the area leaders would be rewarded if their candidate wins. That can be in the form of contracts on community projects in the constituency or a visa to America or the UK.

During the campaigning Spanner would follow Morgie to buy young chicken to give away in return for votes. Sometime it would be Spanner and his son went to buy the chicken and deliver it to the people whose vote it was buying. Morgie don't remember the good his son and Spanner done for him. Most politicians ate their words and promises that they gave out during an election campaign. Spanner and Morgie went to many NEC meeting all over Jamaica during the 1990s.

Spanner house was burned down on the night before the 1993 general election by unscrupulous party supporters because they accused him of spying and being a traitor. Spanner had to run away from Kitson Town, and had to move all over the country to be safe from people who wanted to kill him. After The Doctor lost the election, Spanner continued to campaign with him and Morgie in preparation for the next election to come. Spanner and Jack did a very good job by securing the councillor seat for Morgie which he won but the other three councillors lost to the P.N.P. That gave the JLP a voice in the constituency and a platform to work off.

So West Central St. Catherine was being rule for the first time in 32 years by a P.N.P, MP under a P.N.P government with three PNP councillors. Things got from bad to worst under the P.N.P woman who was the Member of Parliament. For the record West Central St. Catherine is the biggest constituency in Jamaica. The Doctor continued to run his doctor surgery for the constituency, where anyone could get a check up if they were sick and they would be given medicine to get better and discussed constituency matters. Dr Baugh used that tactics well and in the end it paid off but all those millions that he used in the constituency has to be recouping back from somewhere.

That worked well with everyone and they repay him back in the general election where he won convincingly. Even though he did lose before to Barker, he never gives up and he continues to campaign across the constituency for another five years until the election was called. Barker abandons his comrades and, some became hungry and destitute but The Doctor didn't turn them away or accuse them of voting against him. What he did surprise many people, Spanner continued to give out the word to everyone to contact The Doctor at his medical surgery for help? Barker was nowhere to be found so her loyal servant switched on her and voted her out of parliament. Some of the people couldn't afford medication because they didn't have any money to pay. Spanner's was instrumental in orchestrating the plan to get the people on The Doctor's side. Spanner's ambition was to run West Central St Catherine one day as its Member of Parliament, but first he would have to go through the councillor route.

In 2002, another general election was called and The Doctor won the seat that he works so hard for over the years with the help of Spanner and others Labourites. In 2007, he won again but this time his party came into government. He was given the deputy prime minister role and Minister of Foreign Affairs and foreign trades. The J.L.P government was now run by Prime Minister Bruce Golding who attended school with Spanner mother. Bruce's dad taught Spanner's mother at school too. They came from the same community in West Central St. Catherine named Saint Faith, between Macca Tree and Browns Hall district. Spanner said "I saw lots of things during the P.N.P and J.L.P rule but I couldn't stay in Jamaica and say too much because I would be killed. I have an obligation to my country, my people and the world to high light Jamaica's corrupt political system. Who want to be like Salomon Rushdie? Not I so I sprint left Jamaica".

Kitson Town was the headquarters for politics in West Central St. Catherine and Spanner was always in the middle of it. Melvin Woodfine a P.N.P candidate turned councillor was a good man. He got electric light, pipe water and asphalt road in Kitson Town when the J.L.P member of parliament for decade, could not or did not interested. Mrs Bennett the JLP MP at the time congratulated the PNP councillor for getting lights and asphalt road in and around Kitson Town.

After the 1980s election, Spanner didn't take part in anymore politic until 1990 when the P.N.P caretaker Enoch Blake, who was his solicitor, asked for his help. Spanner wasn't a P.N.P, he had just come out of prison, but he was doing Blake a favour because he prevented him from going back to prison, free of charge. Blake knew and heard about Spanner's influences so he did whatever was in his power to have him on his side. Blake was a good P.N.P member but his party leader, gave him a big fight and pushed him out of the caretaker role in West Central St. Catherine of which Kitson Town was his base. May God bless Mr Blake and Vindel Wallace souls.

That was when a woman came in as the P.N.P candidate who went on to won the seat for the first time for the P.N.P in the history of Jamaican politics. The P.N.P general secretary and the minister of security was instrumental in helping her to won the selection for caretaker, because they bring in thugs from Kingston, with police to keep out the delegates who wanted Blake to continued representing the constituency.

They pushed Blake out of the seat and soon after he died. They said that he died of cancer but some maintained it was stress over the way his party had treated him why he died. That was the first time Spanner saw what infighting in the P.N.P or in politics was about.

Spanner was at a meeting when the Prime Minister at the time gave a speech at the national arena about Col Trevor McMillan, who was the police commissioner at the time and doing a fine job, which was irresponsible. Not long after he was push out of the post of commissioner of police. Politics and the security of the nation should never mix. That was the way of politics in Jamaica. They stole poor people's money and enrich themselves and family. They used poor people money that they stole to educate their kids in universities in America and the UK, while the poor can't afford to send their kids to school. How cruel was that?

Spanner said "I remember being told at a PNP conference by two senior ministers in the Patterson Government that the Mormon or (Later Day Saint) was spying for America. They told me that they were sure those so-called Christian are spying on Jamaica. I too believed that they are but if the government has nothing to hide or fear, why worry? If the country is governed well and the so-called leaders get rid of all corruption, there should be nothing to fare America and Britain for?"

Bruce Golding

What were the motives of Bruce Golding in not wanting to sign the extradition papers for Dudus? Don't forget that Golding always associated himself with questionable characters. Take for instance, Jack man who was helping him to change Spanish Town and Homestead into NDM when he switched from the JLP. After a while Jack man couldn't be control and he was murdered by the police extra-judicial style.

The JLP and the PNP were tricked into joining the Euro-American plan to destabilise Jamaica, and have sunken so deep into the pit, that salvation seems impossible to save it. Can Jamaica sink any lower than in the 1980s? Norman and Michael Manley must be turning in their graves because the Dudus saga details suggest that the PNP is now a puppet on a strings. Alas, Jamaica's major political parties are greater enemies of Jamaica than Dudus could ever be. Just look at how the politicians robbed the country of valuable resources for their selfish greed, instead of developing the country for the betterment of its citizens. Hundred of million in US dollars go missing each year from various ministries that cannot be accounted for. Who stole it is anyone guesses.

Which PNP or JLP politician has the guts to put Jamaicans first, including Tivoli Garden residents? None will work for the betterment of Jamaica because if they do they will not be considered important anymore. No wonder the dons are thriving where leadership is lacking, and don't forget that there are many more Tivoli in Jamaica. Jamaica would like to see politicians who can hold up his or her hands and say that he/she is free from the dons and corruption! Are there any politicians in the JLP or PNP who have not sold their souls to dons and gunmen and to the Euro-American terrorists that manipulate them? All Jamaican politicians are puppet to America and Europe. They have to do what these countries asked of them to get money to help the country but when they get it, they robbed most of it.

Let such PNP and JLP persons stand up and counted, or forever shut up and hang their head in shame. Could you imagine what would happen if all dons should decide to sing like a Canary? All Jamaican politicians would have to resign. Golding needs to get his act together or get out of Jamaica House.

Until politicians are ready to tear down their garrisons, which include Portia Simpson Miller, Mike Henry, Babsy Grange, Karl Samuda, Dr Peter Phillips, Omar Davis, Delroy Chuck, Phillip Paulwell, Ronald Thwaites, Anthony Hylton, Sharon Hay Webster, Natalie Hedley, Maurice Guy, Lisa Hanna, Roger Clarke, Andrew Holness, Horace Chang, Bruce Golding and others should not be allowed to take part in the political process. As for now, all hypocrites should be quiet and allow PM Golding to solve the Dudus mess and distraction which he allowed to happen on his watch, maybe now is the time for him to redeem himself and set an example. In the Manley years, there were many Judas Jamaicans among the private sector, churches, media, and other island entities. Are they still there? Every Jamaican at home and abroad must analyse the Dudus tragedy, and work for peace and prosperity, but no one should excuse the real enemies of Jamaica. They are the corrupt politicians, police, civil servants, businessmen, women and so-called dons. Maybe Bruce Golding could now change from Saul to Paul and don't get side tract on his way to Damascus?

Spanner declared: "I love my beautiful country, Jamaica but I despise all politicians including West Central St Catherine past and present MPs. The present deputy Prime Minister who I used to campaign with is a skillful politician. Giving out free medical check up to the people is a cover for the bigger picture. I knew the amount of millions it cost to run the campaign as a caretaker, with the entire vote bought. So can someone tell me where that money came from, and how will it be paid back. MPs pay isn't that much, so that money will have to be taken from somewhere for repayment, that will come from the taxpayers of course. I did have respect for my caretaker, now MP but not anymore. After the defending of Golding in the Dudus saga on TV, he lost all respect from the Jamaican people. The fact of the matter is that all of the politicians are corrupt.

Spanner often questioned the power that is in Jamaica: "I think Jamaica should capitalise on the many varieties of fruit that are wasted each year by processing the fruits for export. That would enable the rural communities to earn valuable foreign exchange which would help the Jamaican economy and the people who sells the fruits. Maybe we could start with a mango festival where there could be a mango eating contest and the judging of the best variety and sweetest mangoes? This could bring in more tourists to the island and generate much needed foreign exchange to the country. Too many fruits go to waste each year without a solution to remedy the problem. Why not export the fruits or make factories to produce fruit juices?" No fruits should be wasted, if it can't make juices, then make vinegar with it. There is a market also for the by-products of the fruits which is making animals feed. Problems solved.

Spanner said "I am not trying to inflate the matter but it's the truth. At some stage of my life, I have lived in all fourteen parishes and I have spent some time with my fishermen friends 'Clive' aka Enus over Port Royal too. I am qualified to speak on matter of corruption and all the ills that happen in Jamaica involving politicians, public officials, police and dons. No one can question my honesty on the topic because I have lived and seen it with my two eyes. In Jamaica police and politicians are the most corrupt in society. People would want to believe and put their trust in these public servants, but they shouldn't be trusted. There are people in the civil service who hold on to respective ministries as their turf and will victimise member of the opposition, both political parties done it".

Spanner continued "I was a political activist on all three sides. I was a JLP, PNP and NDM supporter during my 32 years of active politicking. I knew area leaders and businessmen and women and politicians in all sixty constituencies and at some time or another I visited and did some campaigning for them. My involvement in politics gives me the opportunity to know all the politicians past and present who were involved in wrong doings. Some of those politicians were worst than the gunmen, because they are the ones who gave the gunmen money to buy the guns and ammunition in the first place. I knew a few policemen who were involved in selling guns and bullets to gunmen. Some of those policemen would inform the gunmen when there was a raid planned and they give out the names of informants who gave information to them. In Guanaboa Vale there were two policemen there who used to loan out their guns to criminals and one used to give Spanner friend gunshot for his gun".

He continued "some of the businessmen and women are to be blame too. Some of the so-called community leaders are the ones who finance the gangs to buy ammunitions to kill poor people. All the big businesses have gunmen who they pay to protect them and their businesses. No politicians can look me in the eye and tell me that they are clean and immune from corruption. Being corrupt comes with the territory. For instance young lawyers will get a caretaker role for a constituency. What will happen is that maybe this person is a novice or a pro in politricks. This is what will happen: the boldest area leaders will go to that caretaker office to see him and let him know who they are. Those area leaders are the ones who have the guns, command all the power and have greatest influence.

Furthermore "this caretaker politician may be a Christian and most likely from a good upbringing but niceness don't win election, so this is where the gangs and hoodlums come in. The area leaders are the ones who talk strategy with the politicians on how to win their seat in an election. For all the advice and support they give the politicians they would have to start hand out large amounts of cash to these people on a weekly basis. The caretakers want to be MP so they will do anything to get into Gordon House (Parliament) and once they reach Parliament all the money spent will be recovered and more. Politics is business, and you would be surprised to see what people do, just to be a politician because they feel it's their license to steal and get rich".

Spanner said "I knew that in rural constituencies, on most occasions, the caretakers or sitting MP would import gunmen from the city who were supporters of their party to intimidate their opponents. It's a way of life in Jamaican politics and it needs to be eradicated. When the PNP woman caretaker was getting resistance from Spanner and other area leaders, Zekes and a few of his men were brought in from Matthews Lane to intimidate the guys but no one was afraid of him or his men because many guns were at the area leader's disposal to take care of any problems.

Don't watch the foreign observers who visit the country when there is an election, to monitor the results. They can't see the organisational work that's done underground. Even the CIA plays its role in the election by financing and sabotaging of the outcomes. I was paid to steal ballot boxes and to intimidate my opponents. Many of my politics friends who are area leaders were involved in that practice. I have seen people being beaten up, house burnt down, and notice given out for opponent to leave their area".

He continued "all those things went on while corrupt cops who are working with the MPs or caretakers turned a blind eye to what was happening. Many times people begged for their lives and properties to be spared but it fell on deaf ears. Every politician has some notorious characters that support their election campaign. If the politician refuse to associate with that person and that person had lots of influence in the constituency, it could cause the politician to lose the election. If the politician is very influential, say he/she is the security minister, then that MP may use the police and soldiers to put pressure on the don, he may even be killed. The don may kill a few of the area leaders who took side with the MP or caretakers too. That would piss off the politician and that's when he set up the don life by getting him killed.

Spanner continued "there were many things a don could do in a constituency, he could change to the other party and most likely the people under his influence would follow him to the other side. No politicians want that to happen so he/she would pay up. But don't forget that the first chance the politician get to bump off the don, they will. The politician only way out of a situation like that was to get the don killed. Occurrences like that happen many times when politicians can't control their dons. It's sometimes hard to prove that the politicians get someone killed because the politician may used one of his same area don to do the job or use the police. With all the cash that the politician had, no one is willing to be a witness."

Spanner continued "while campaigning I was given thousand of dollar to hand out to people who didn't want to vote or who needed it the most. I used to distribute my money fairly. Sometimes, I would go to a house whose household was so poor that I had to buy cooking oil, salt, flour, cornmeal, milk, bread, chicken back, salted fish, hair oil, lotion and kerosene oil. That method was used as a way to buy vote. If it wasn't for the election no one would remember those poor old souls. Sometimes I would stop in the town centre (square) and I would buy drinks for everyone which could easily be over a hundred people. The car that I travelled in was paid for by the politician, who gave me the money to buy vote. Some of those people were the poorest of the constituency who needed help but the politicians just used them. After the politician won his or her seat in parliament, most time they didn't come around until the next election.

Then on Election Day some of the old folks have to be lifted up out of their beds and transported to the polling stations to cast their vote, and the politicians turn round ignoring them after he won. Those bastard don't have any heart, they only love their family and don't cares for the people who put them in power. When political activists get too powerful the politicians always get them killed by using the police or soldiers to get rid of them. Two famous Tivoli Garden dons, and Jackman from Homestead in Spanish Town and all those guys who got killed in the 'Green Bay' affair, were the works of politicians using the State security agents to murdered people they can't control anymore. Most of the famous cops in Jamaica have a manual on how to execute so-called don and gunmen without being charge or going to prison for their crime. Most time when the politicians used gunmen to do their killing, the politicians would have to get rid of the hit man by getting him killed too. Or maybe the gunman then goes to the United States, UK or Canada and became a big drugs don".

Them versus Us

The British government don't like anything from Jamaica because they are saying that Jamaicans are in the same group as the Taliban, Sudanese, Iraqis and Algerians. That means Jamaicans are class as terrorists by the British, because they can't push Jamaican around. To go to Europe, Jamaicans have to get a visa from the British High Commission in Kingston, for an in transit flight through the UK. In 2003 during the Patterson government the UK imposed visa restrictions on Jamaica and our 'yes man' government did nothing about it. Spanner asked "why the Jamaican government didn't slap back visa restrictions on British Citizens who are not related to nor have Jamaican relatives or connection? Spanner said "Speaking to Dr Baugh who is the Minister of Foreign Affair and deputy PM, on the topic of deportation the other day and he couldn't give me a good argument on the subject. He sounds like Jamaican politicians have to lick ass and get all the abuse just to get aid from some foreign government. He was telling me that he couldn't do anything for deportees, then why accept them in the country then"?

"He was too scared of upsetting the British whose handout the government depend on". Spanner continued "I noticed that the UK government has given some small change toward rehabilitating deportees but the government is doing different things with the money. By doing that the money can be easily siphon off into someone pockets. One senior superintendent of police even commented against deportee getting reintegration money to start their life over after being deported. That was pure bad-mind on the part of the cop because he stated that giving deportee's money would be saying to them that crime pays. What that cop didn't realise is that once deportees don't have anything to do, it will lead them to crime and that would be more pressure on the police with their limited resources and the country".

Taking on the colonial master

It should be remembered that during slavery, Nanny Jamaica's only female heroine and her brave warriors, killed lots of British soldiers and slave masters and burned down their great houses and cane fields. On many occasions the slaves defeated the white slave masters and hence they had a thing about Jamaican nationals. It's a fact that in the UK Jamaicans get the worst treatment out of all nationalities and yet they expect that their citizens should be treated with respect when they travel to Jamaica.

By burning down the slave masters mansions and killing many soldiers, it sent shockwaves all over Britain. The world now knows that they can't mess with a Jamaican even when that person isn't a criminal, we just don't take any nonsense from anyone. Jamaica is a small nation but we are not afraid to defend our rights and that's what will happen because the British and American governments take Jamaicans for idiot but we are not. Spanner said "I hated bullies and that's what America and England authorities are".

The Jamaican government needs to tell the US and UK to fuck off out of its internal affairs. The dons were saying that if they caught any white men or women who looked suspicious in their area or communities they would kill them. Spanner asked "so what if those governments send black people knowing the fact that Jamaica is a black country? Would the black agents be seen as the enemies too? Brando replied "They would have to be eliminated just like the pigs they are". Spanner didn't support the killing of innocent people. Some of these people were spies who were helping to sabotage the government and they couldn't see it. Spanner said "so as a citizen of Jamaica I will defend my country from the politicians who are selling us out to the US and UK, who are out to destroy the Jamaican people". It was after the US involvement in Jamaican politics and internal affairs that cocaine was introduced into the country. They introduced it to Jamaica, and now they were putting Jamaicans in prison for trafficking or selling it to the US and UK".

Bang the hit man

Here was a guy who was a P.N.P enforcer and hit man, and the former Security Minister was the lawyer who always defended him on all his murder cases. Spanner knew bang very well even though he didn't like him, and at one stage they were at the General Penitentiary together during the 1980s. Bang always got off his many murders using this skilful lawyer who later turned politician and security minister. Bang killed one of Spanner's friends Stinky, because he lost a gun he loaned him. Bang was from Manchester, but he ruled Samakan a community, in the Seaward Drive area of Kingston 11, with an iron fist.

His control wasn't going to last forever, because some of the youths who were friends of Spanner and Stinky paid him a visit one night and gave him 17 shot killing him on the spot. They had to do it because Bang would get them killed and get away with it too, so they made sure to get rid of the garbage. He was buried in the rural district of Christiana in Spaulding in the parish of Manchester and that was the end of another murderous don. Bang had been a hit man for many politicians and business people. This politician was more conning than a fox but most of all he was a criminal hiding behind the lawyer suit and as a politician. Spanner "I could go on and on but in Jamaica there was always someone to get you kill if you know and talk too much and that was one of the reasons why I had to leave Jamaica".

The many gifts

Trinity used to send load of Italian suits, top of the line leather shoes, fine jewellery which included watches, rings, bracelets, cuff links and chains for his politician's friends and associate. Other goodies include briefcases, nice pens, expensive mobile phones and loads of cash to those corrupted cops and politicians. Trinity used to be a political activist for the JLP during the 1970s, and he wasn't the kind of person who would forget where he was coming from. They were politicians and cops who he respected, maybe they were cops who he used to paid bribes or politicians who he used to rigged votes and fire shots for, I don't know but I do knew he did sent them gifts.

The dons would remember the favour from the politicians, so they would send gifts in the form of flashy cars, clothes, money and jewellery. Sometimes the politicians are the ones who launder the drugs money for the dons. There are also some top notch gunmen who are gay and politicians have sex with them and give them visa to leave Jamaica. Some of those guys in the crowd would kill a batty boy (gay) if they see one of them being mob on the street but behind closed door they are the ones who giving away their bottom and giving blow jobs for visa. Spanner believed that some of those so-called bad boys were secret gays or rather wolves in sheep clothing....*The End*

Books to come by Clifton Cameron

My First Fix- Novel
My Inheritance- Children and adult story
Fluffy- Children story
Indefinite Detention-Human Rights in the UK
Auto-Biography
The forgotten one- a collection of poems
Crying out loud- a book of short stories
Please check out the author website at: http://www.jamrock-promotion-and-sales.com
On Twitter: chiston2008 and Face book: Clifton Cameron
This book is written using a mixture of everyday Jamaican language and terminology, and plain English.

Terms like 'likkle but wi tallawa' simple means 'small but strong'. 'Jah-mek-ya' means 'Jamaica'. 'Politricks' means 'cunning politicians or politics'. How-di-do, meaning hello or how are you doing? Dem: simple meaning 'them'. Mi: means 'me'. Draws: meaning 'panty or knickers'. Wid: means 'with'. Wi: means 'we'. Jam Down: means 'Jamaica'. Jam Rock: means 'Jamaica'. Dat: means 'that'. Sanki: means 'singing a hymn'. Tun: means 'turn'. Yuh: means 'you or yours'. Mek: means 'make'. Salt ting: means 'salt fish, salt mackerel, salt beef, salt herring or any meat kind'. Nuh means don't or not. As for Traficater it means someone who traffic stuff, a smuggler.